PESSIMISM

PESSIMISM

JOE BAILEY

Routledge
LONDON & NEW YORK

First published in 1988 by
Routledge
11 New Fetter Lane, London EC4P 4EE

Published in the USA by
Routledge Inc.
in association with Methuen Inc.
29 West 35th Street, New York, NY 10001

Set in Plantin Light
by Pentacor Ltd
High Wycombe, Bucks
and printed in Great Britain
by T.J. Press (Padstow) Ltd
Padstow, Cornwall

Library of Congress Cataloging in Publication Data

Bailey, Joe.
    Pessimism/Joe Bailey.
        p.   cm.
    Bibliography: p.
    Includes index.
    1. Pessimism.   2. Social movements.   I. Title.
HM291.B22 1988
302.5—dc19   87–15756
                                          CIP

British Library CIP Data also available
ISBN 0415 00247 8 (c)
ISBN 0415 00248 6 (pb)

CONTENTS

PREFACE AND ACKNOWLEDGMENTS

Pessimism is a peculiar idea. It is either seen as a psychological problem or as a metaphysical issue, but in neither sense is it treated as useful or illuminating or in any way relevant to our understanding of the world. It is the thesis of this book that pessimism and optimism are unavoidable kinds of social judgment of the future which we all display and act upon. Both professional and popular views of what is likely to happen to our societies are redolent with these judgments which are turning, increasingly, to the pessimistic.

Feeling pessimistic and gloomy is not some kind of aberration if there are good grounds for it. Making these feelings marginal and even irrelevant to social thought is to neglect important data, especially if we can point to variations in the intensity of pessimism. If we can see good reasons for the dominance of gloomy views of the future the risk of increasing the sense of foreboding should not inhibit us from linking what we think and feel with what we can see happening. Yet there is a strong sense that pessimism paralyses, that it is a celebration of passiveness and that it can do no good to dwell on what *could*, even what is *likely* to happen.

I have tried to show that such a self-protective and wilful ignorance cannot be justified, at the very least because pessimism, as a form of *social* thought, cannot be ignored. Further I have tried to suggest that there are good reasons for this pessimism. The major grounds are the fixity and immutability of our social relations, rather than simply technological developments. The risks of nuclear war, increasing hunger and gross environmental pollution are only assessable in the light of the apparent inability of our societies to modify their social organisation when faced with new potentials for damage. This is not to say that there are no signs of hope, but that they face social processes which seem massively immobile.

Chapter 1 outlines the current increase in pessimism. Chapter 2 describes why feelings are an important part of social consciousness in general and of pessimism in particular. Chapter 3 raises pessimism as a viable intellectual construct, particularly for sociology. Chapter 4 describes the rise and fall of the idea of progress. Chapter 5 looks at utopias as revealing indicators of optimism and pessimism. The remainder of the book gives some justifications for the current social pessimism which has been elaborated conceptually in the first section. Chapter 6 examines some of the implications of the forecasting and futurology which we have become familiar with over the last two decades. Chapter 7 tries to map the dimensions, if not the details, of the most serious reason for pessimism; the nuclear arms race. Chapter 8 attempts to sketch the same for two other major problems, food and nuclear energy. Chapter 9 interrogates the 'new' politics and social movements as a basis for hope.

My conviction that pessimism is a powerful form of social consciousness took root in 1983 when I was fortunate enough to be a visiting lecturer at the University of Konstanz. I returned there two years later to give a lecture course on the topic. The students demonstrated that it was possible to be both sociologically pessimistic and personally hopeful. I am particularly grateful to Professor Heinrich Mäding for making these visits possible and for the personal hospitality he and Heidrun showed me. Additionally I must thank Christian Egenhoffer, Gaby Jauernig, and Jurgen Janovsky for their kindness and support. I have become exceptionally boring about pessimism in my own institution and the forebearance of colleagues in the School of Sociology, Kingston Polytechnic should be mentioned. I am most grateful to Caro Bailey for showing me the full implications of seeing the glass as half full rather than as half empty.

This book is about the future and is for Josh and Anna.

CHAPTER 1

A NEW SENSE OF DANGER

It is now difficult to be optimistic. In general conversation, in journalism, in popular social commentary, in political argument, in academic social analysis, perhaps in art, literature and general works of the imagination there are few signs of hope about the future. It is not just that the political vocabulary of us all is dominated by 'crisis', 'emergency', 'danger', 'dilemma' or whatever, though it probably is, at least in newspaper and TV news coverage – perhaps it always was.[1] For some time now it has been remarked that 'crisis' is a mundane element in our thought[2] and to that extent it has soaked into our conversation and thereby been drained of its power to alarm us. We have got used to talking as though the future is not only provisional but is dominated by dangers rather than opportunities.

Is this remarkable? Is it simply that there is rather more public talking and writing than there was and that the existential anxieties of all men and women in all times (and perhaps all places) are amplified now by the powerful media of their communication?[3] From this viewpoint hope and despair about the future are fairly constantly mixed in social life and imbalances are local, short-lived and may even be constructed out of the self-interests and influence of particular social groups – such as sociologists.[4]

A lot of social science has taken on the task of describing new and alarming social problems and then, later, showing them to be artificially publicised and that what we took to be new social phenomena were really only the refractions of the same old fears dramatised with new costumes and props to new audiences. A smug knowingness results from this cycle of panic followed by scepticism which embodies the view that there is nothing new under the sun, that our society is fundamentally the same as all others, that history repeats itself (or, as Voltaire would have it, at least men do) and that we should not become too excited. The popular version of this is that there are no social arrangements which are unchangeable. In short human nature remains the same and so, therefore, does society.

From this assumption it becomes an act of hubris to try and describe directions of social change and, consequently, to even indicate the effects of such shifts on social consciousness. The future is unknowable and therefore general social expectations of that future as well as professional 'futurology' are fictions and fantasies which may be interesting in their own right but are irrelevent to that future. In the strongest version of this perspective the construction of views of the future can have totalitarian consequences through the self-fulfillment of politics itself.[5]

Social science, then, should not participate in such panics about the future. It cannot sound alarm bells itself and it should not act as the herald for the fears of others.

This leaves us with the issue of how social science is to express the intense concern with the future which is an obvious characteristic of modern consciousness. It shares with the society of which it is a part an intellectual curiosity about and an emotional longing for the future.

The intellectual curiosity, for sociologists at least, is seen in the attempt to embody the possibilities and potentials of social change in their commentary upon the present. The future (and also the past) *is* part of the present. It is embedded in present culture in the form of predictions, prophecies, forecasts and extrapolations which, essentially, reorder our present arrangements in desired or feared ways. Thus our culture both values present social realities and refashions them *in theory* by using the future as an intellectual tool.

The emotional longing for the future is more complicated to express clearly because our view of 'feelings' can conventionally only be understood as individual expressions. Yet the meaning of feelings is socially defined and their provocation and the manner of their formulation can only be understood in relation to social conditions. We have hopes and fears about what will or might happen to us as a society, as well as individuals, which are very powerful and which engage some of the deepest senses of the significance of our lives. These shared feelings about the future also have an effect on our actions in the present.

Given these two profound attachments to the future we cannot deny it as an object of study. This, presumably, explains why the future has always been such a major concern in social science in spite of logical objections to its status. What, then, is to be studied?

Given the unknowable nature of what *will* happen all that can be studied is what *could* happen, and through this, two things: the general sense or consciousness of what could happen, and the fatefulness of particular kinds of thing that are happening, that is the links between what is happening now and what could happen in the future.

These present two valuable tasks for the sociologist. The first concerns the social state of mind about the future and how diverse publics, notably through their writings, imagine and judge possible futures, the unanimity and diversity of these images, their sources and, especially, their consequences for attitudes and thus for social action. In particular can we trace changes in the general judgments made about the future? Does the future appear to be different now than it did, say a generation ago?

The second task requires that we go beyond simply mapping changes in social consciousness (difficult as this alone is) to describe the altering possibilities of social change. The future which we experience now is not composed of an ever-expanding list of alternative directions which could be taken. Possibilities are not expanded additively in some way, but are socially structured. Particular changes in the past and present *destroy* alternatives for ever and appear to become massive determinisms in their own right. For instance the existence of nuclear weaponry or nuclear energy cannot be 'disinvented' or forgotten and these developments themselves create possibilities for the future which exclude other avenues – that is reliance on conventional warfare to settle disputes or on 'safe' energy sources. So what could happen in the future has a 'shape' which can be described and judged now. This is not the same thing as saying, for example, that we are all going to hell in a handcart but that hell is now a possible direction and that this particular handcart is absorbing all our economic, political and cultural resources and that other kinds of transport to different destinations seem to be monopolised by only cranky passengers who are labelled as deluded, utopian or even malicious by our leaders. So I intend to open up these two tasks for further discussion; to describe the changing form of our cultural understanding of the future and to relate this understanding to objective possibilities – and especially dominant dangers – for our future.

The overall tenor of this discussion is pervaded, at present, by a sense of foreboding and fear, by an apprehension that we are in a position of potential danger which is not a perpetual or even recurrent feature of social thought and which is not a projection of inner anxiety, however derived, on to history.[6] Since the invention and use of nuclear weapons our potential future has changed. But more than this the modern period has, perhaps partly as a result of the anxiety about this development, elaborated such a sophisticated form of monitoring and self-conscious judgment of its own performance that we are now more aware than ever before of the dangers we run. We think, write and talk in a world which reverberates with both explosions and with the description of those explosions. Never before has there been such a significance of reports in both senses of the word.

There is a new sense of danger, a sense of a worsening which may stretch from the exhaustion of our previous confidence in progress to a paralysing desperation. It is audible and legible but it is not yet clearly dominant. It is probably stronger among those groups which professionally construct and debate social thought such as academics and journalists. Yet it is more extensive than this. It is relatively novel, though the experience of my generation, growing up after World War II, may have led to a misleading sense of rapid decline and disappointment. It seems to have grown stronger over the last few years. Most important of all it seems to be justifiable or, at least, grounded in accelerating political and technological processes.

The term I wish to apply to this sense of increasing difficulty is 'pessimism' and, by historical as well as lexical contrast, 'optimism'. These terms are used in everyday life but have rarely been seen as illuminating in sociology. I hope to show that they light up a hitherto obscured and confused area of our social thought which has been too intricately bound up with our feelings to be easily probed. Indeed the routinisation of our sense of hopelessness into a facet of personality or into a metaphysical taste or, as seems more usual among social scientists, into an ironic defence for avoiding judgments which are, in turn, marginalised as 'emotional', is itself a marker of an area of unease.

But these terms – pessimism and optimism – can have perfectly respectable mundane meanings which refer to people's shared judgments about the supposed direction of social change on criteria which can be made explicit. These judgments have powerful social and cultural effects in that they lead to the formation of social movements and social organisations to affect these issues, or, alternatively, to justify apathy and inertia. That they have moral and emotional resonances is a signal of their salience in our social life, not a reason for avoiding them as in some way tainted by inappropriate value judgments. After all what is at issue here is a matter of feelings and values experienced and acted upon in the process of creating social change. Pessimism is the name we give to our gloomy expectations, to our self-conscious engagement in our own fears and dreads about what might occur. It is about our trepidations and our social valuations.

There is a difficulty in talking and writing on this topic that one becomes a Jeremiah. The rhetorical flourishes of doomsaying and gloom-spreading are, in a perverse way, attractive in that they imply a clearly settled and finalised view of our ends. This dissolves doubt in the very passion of public despair. However the fatalism of the millenarian, the eschatologist and the disaster-merchant leads his or her audience only to the masochistic celebration of 'the end'. Such an anticipation is entirely pathological. It forecloses the main possibility which can be the obvious outcome of such anxieties, namely that we take heed and change direction. One of the peculiarities of the present form of pessimism is that it is so all-knowing and complacent in its confidence and its pretence to rationality that it seems to paralyse the will.[7] Its basis in science,[8] its scanning of the empirical facts, in short its avoidance of the other-worldly or transcendental character of past pessimisms make it a tricky topic to analyse with a constructive intention. What is the point of describing the extent and penetration of pessimism in our society, and, even more dubiously, how justified it is? There are two general answers to this question.

First, there is nothing finally determined about our future. We still have choices to make which are socially structured and informed. Part of the information we use is that about our own understanding of our dangers and our intellectual and emotional connection with what we think might lie ahead. This reflexive, self-referential understanding is part of the task of the social disciplines. George Orwell, towards the end of the Second World War, remarked that a picture of the future was a condition of our ability to make rational choices.[9] Ignoring how we socially construct our image of the future and, particularly, how we evaluate and feel about it contributes to our irrationality which, given the present dangers, may be a terminal form of ignorance. The nuclear arms race, increasing technological determination of social processes, the abuse of nature, mutual predation between nations, the collapse of a culture of experience into one of consumption, mounting relative deprivation and so on and on. All of these are now newly dangerous and some are clearly potentially terminal for the social world as we can imagine it. Yet none are in principle uncontrollable and the view that they are so, in practice, is the most dangerous contribution to their instabilities.

The second answer is that making an implicit pessimism explicit contributes to the stock of knowledge. Far from reinforcing our nearly-suppressed anxieties (and also our own fears about our fears), explicating the hidden is a way of changing this knowledge. E.P. Thompson speaks of the danger of a 'subliminal teleology', of a hidden level of 'inertial push' which denies and destroys our power to make choices.[10] It is the assumed, half-conscious, dimly perceived, taken-for-granted character of our pessimism which damps down the heat of alternative goal-setting and which supplies the cynicism which in its turn condemns as 'utopian' all attempts to unite criticism with constructive alternatives.

These two answers to the convinced secular pessimist are given in peculiar circumstances. The present period is unlike any other in three particular respects. There has never been, objectively, such potential danger for the human species; there has never been, subjectively, such a well distributed understanding of that danger; there is, now, a fully realised record of the failure of our societies to deal with that danger. The modern world gives substance and form to pessimistic expectations as never before.

It is difficult to avoid a rhetorical 'hyping', a preaching and sermonising tone in these circumstances.[11] Listing the dangers we face has itself a deadening effect. It becomes a litany which is only half listened to because it seems so familiar. We are bombarded constantly with these problems so that they become, in all their intractability, part of the background. This certainly has psychological effects visible in the personal strategies we use to avoid what is not, but what becomes the unthinkable.[12] Penetrating this carapace of protective indifference for the mass of people is a matter of great importance and great difficulty. It is an easier task to address specialist audiences through formal education and the public forums for serious debate. The tone adopted, however, is crucial as the psychological and, especially, emotional defences against despair understandably forbid a full acceptance of the present dangers, at least in a non-religious way. The sense of survival while we are, as Aronson describes it, 'living on the brink',[13] requires that we focus on this side of the abyss where everything still seems solid and stable. The tone, then, should be one which sees our predicament from *terra firma*, which knows that this is where we are and can remain but which creeps right up to the edge, not to peer fearfully over but to stare long and hard downward and then to gaze back to look for the most secure ground.

CHAPTER 2

THE SOCIAL STATE OF MIND

One of the principal objections to taking pessimism seriously as a concept is that it is drenched in *feelings*. Yet this is its very salience for us. It is important to consider the relevance of feelings, and the emotions in general, to social consciousness before we look at pessimism in particular.

SOCIAL CONSCIOUSNESS AND STATE OF MIND

What we think and how we think are both social. This banal statement, accepted without question by all apprentice social scientists, sometimes seems to close off more sensible speculation than it promotes, partly because it is so obvious and partly because the contrast between 'thought' and 'the social' seems to be so comprehensive as to say all that can be said. Thinking is what we do that makes us human; society is where we do it which makes us social. Connecting the two is what is important. What more need be said?

But this task falls into three parts: examining *how* we think – not just the processes of cognition but describing what thinking means; describing *what* is thought – the 'primitive' object of thought; describing *how* the process of thinking affects what is thought about and vice versa. Phrased like this such a project looks impossibly profound and philosophical though a great deal of phenomenological inquiry has been devoted to making precisely such questions empirical through the study of language and other forms of communication.[1]

My intention is to add to the debate by augmenting the idea of 'social thought' with a stress on the importance of emotion and feeling. I want to show that forms of thought may embody kinds of feeling, pleasurable and painful, and that this provides significant motivational power to thought. Often social thought is treated as an analogue of cognition which is itself seen by sociologists as something similar to what they themselves do or, alternatively, as somehow non-rational and therefore inferior.[2]

The importance of this for pessimism and optimism as evaluations of the future is obvious, namely that judging what could happen is drenched with feelings which may themselves redirect thought and also channel it towards action or inaction. I am not suggesting that emotion is some sort of addition to thinking, some sort of overlay, but that it is, to a greater or lesser extent, part of it. We think and feel at the same time. Pessimism, as a form of thought which may be individually felt as well as expressed, but which has social shape and form, is a profoundly upsetting kind of apprehension which is why it may be marginalised and avoided in analysis and in everyday life. It may be a kind of social thought which is peculiarly resonant with bad feelings, but to some degree all forms of thought are characterised in this way. Academic sociology has sometimes acknowledged this. For instance the relevance of 'alienation' following Marx, and 'anomie' following Durkheim and 'non-rational action' following Weber are not lessened by the emotional valencies these have both for the analyst and the social subject experiencing them. But neither have these qualities of feeling been explored or assessed as essential components of the concepts in question, as part of what makes them revealing or fertile for the social commentator. The emotional salience of concepts remains a ghost or shadow character, secretly essential to their value but regarded widely as unrespectable.

How then do we refer to social consciousness? The first thing to be said is that there is a very impressive range of concepts used to capture the full significance of social consciousness and especially of its essential duality as, on the one hand, experienced and displayed *individually* and, on the other, as socially shared. Culture, sensibility, ideology, beliefs and belief systems, attitudes, opinions and world views . . . are all terms familiar in the conceptual commentary on social consciousness. These terms are used within the core, unresolvable, constitutive frame of reference of sociology, namely the indissoluble connection between the material and the ideal. That is, the world is composed of objective, physical constraints of space, time and resources and of the simultaneous subjective social meaning of those constraints. The social subject within this dualism is both a collective and an individual subject. But it is the individual who can be said in any meaningful sense to experience social consciousness and also to *feel*.[3] To grasp this ontological priority, to rip the idea of social consciousness from its felt aspects and graft it onto the collective subject so that social groups can be said to exhibit social consciousness in the form of social thought, this has required that the emotional dimensions of that experience be cut away. Although we may be happy with the idea that whole societies can, somehow, evince ideologies, belief systems or *Weltanschauungen*, we are, wrongly in my view, less happy with the idea that they can display characteristic forms of feeling. Some writers on culture, especially Raymond Williams,[4] have certainly tried to see modes of feeling and sensibility as an essential part of culture. The real attraction of imaginative literature and art for social science is as a source of feeling.[5] But, in the main, it is ignored at the social level or just read off in a crude positive/negative way as a sort of 'charge' of the form of thought, like the voltage of an electrical current. In this sense the convenient tripartite distinction between cognition, emotion and action sees emotion as a sort of dynamo, almost literally a motive power.[6]

We deal with social consciousness, analytically, in sociology in two distinct ways. The first is exemplified in the recent work of Anthony Giddens.[7] He casts the human agent in social analysis as a set of consciousnesses which are essentially individual capacities to *know* and which is derived from a development of Freud's view of consciousness. Giddens sees consciousness as threefold; first, 'practical consciousness'; – know-how, tacit stocks of knowledge used in constructing social activity; next, 'discursive consciousness' – discourse, talk *about* know-how; last, 'unconscious knowledge' which involve 'desire' (which is not the same as emotion) but is also a form of cognition. These forms of consciousness are all treated as knowledge which is specifically differentiated from 'belief', and from which emotion or feeling is absent as an actual component or a relevant analytical term. Social consciousness is, in turn, read off from the social individual but it is only seen as cognition, and cognition is seen as a *practice* or an *agency* which reproduces social structure and is, in turn, produced by it. Social consciousness, in Giddens' view, in some sense 'fits' and recursively plays back the world of space, time and resources. If it involves a mode of experience we wish to call feeling it only does so in a way which, presumably, lubricates this process or, at most, charges it with the necessary motivational significance. There is plainly room here, in Giddens' work, for the examination of the form and function of social emotion.

The second way we have dealt with social consciousness in social science is less thoughtful and analytic. This is by treating consciousness as simply its *products* which can be empirically collected by the researcher. This leads to a mapping of stratified levels of forms of thought. We see, essentially, two levels, mass consciousness – shared and largely unquestioned attitudes and opinions which can be polled[8] – and specialist ideologies. The latter are the structured beliefs and values specific to, and functional for, particular social locations such as occupations, age grades, genders, social classes, etc. The most well-known example of such a treatment is the description by Mannheim of 'utopias' and 'ideologies'.[9] These world views are seen as characteristic forms of social thought which make sense of, justify and generally 'fit' the political position of particular groups. The whole 'sociology of knowledge' tradition treats social consciousness as sets of ideas which can only make sociological sense if understood as the productions of groups which are themselves seen as sharing interests or positions.[10]

Both of these ways of understanding social consciousness are useful but they share the omission of experienced feeling as a dimension of that consciousness.

The notion of 'social state of mind' has a more inclusive hold on social consciousness. The idea may seem vague or indeterminate but its virtue is that it is not restricted to cognition alone and that it implies a felt condition to a way of thinking. It is close to Williams' idea of society as 'a way of life'. He exploits the attention being paid to the 'new social movements' and to a new form of consciousness which does not contrast emotion and intelligence but 'where people actually live, what is specialized as "emotional" has an absolute and primary significance.'[11] The separation between the two, he says, is the consequence of a deformed social order. Similar preoccupations can be seen in variously expressed ways in a number of 'critical theorists', particularly in the work of Habermas.[12] This gives some conceptual status to individual feeling as a primary mode of experiencing the world without losing the social and therefore variable basis of that feeling. It begins to account for the importance of a form of thought for its thinkers beyond its functionality or its rationality according to some donated criterion.

LOCATIONS OF THE SOCIAL STATE OF MIND: THE PSYCHOLOGICAL AND THE SOCIAL

What has been said implies that there is a disconnection between the social and the psychological levels of the social state of mind which is unnecessary. At the least it implies that there may be absolute, individually – perhaps biologically – determined forms of emotion which put limits upon the feeling involved in social thought. This view – that feeling is really non-social and that this is why it has been ignored by sociology – is mistaken and rests upon a view of psychology which is heavily organismic. Sociology is both frightened and contemptuous of any acceptance of the biological determination of social life and often sees this as the theoretical core of psychology.

It may be helpful to look at these two disconnected levels of the social state of mind – the psychological and the social – in general and in relation to pessimism.

Sociological attempts to deal with states of mind characteristically treat them as properties of collectivities, expressed in group contexts either by formal productions, such as writings, or other public communications. These expressions are seen not *as* states of mind but as *indexes* of them. Cultural analysis follows in which uniformities and variations in these indexes are plotted against changes in the surrounding social conditions.[13] The systematic, organised and coherent quality of such forms of thought are inferred as ideologies or whatever and these are taken to exist as real entities with determining power in their own right. They can be described as systems of ideas with which individuals can engage. But this engagement is in a sense motiveless. That is, the emotional gratifications or pains of believing the ideology – thinking the whole system of ideas – are regarded as only individually variable or even as obvious in relation to social position.

Thus, for example, some writers treat pessimism as the property of particular groups of marginal intellectuals who are seen as the carriers of anxiety and alarm and who panic as their own links to society crumble under the impact of changes which will promote others.[14] Sociology itself has been seen as a good example of this with its recent stress on crisis and imminent breakdown. Noble sees the disastrism and apocalypticism of many social scientists as a property of the analysis itself.[15] There are well known historical studies which see millenarian and apocalyptic beliefs as explained by the social position of their believers.[16] The emotional conditions and consequences of such eschatologies are ignored in spite of the obvious puzzle of how such personally destructive beliefs can be held by those who choose to remain alive. A recourse to categories of 'irrationality', 'collective insanity', 'contagious panic' and the like explain away this issue as a residue in a category of its own and not really part of the historical problem.[17]

Accounts of modern protest movements often focus on their 'expressive' characteristic.[18] This is as far as conventional sociology will allow the dimension of emotion to intrude into analysis. The term 'expressive', rather like 'affective', is used as a half-way house between 'instrumental' and 'irrational'. It is a clear signal that the sociological understanding of states of mind cannot ignore emotions but has given little thought to what they might mean.

This leaves us with the problems of data and method. What are to be regarded as reliable products or indicators of states of mind? How is the emotional – the affective or expressive – to be studied? What are we to look at as the evidence of pessimism?

Psychologists have been much more active with regard to the emotions as an object of study. But just as sociology wishes to absorb the psychological as given in its approach, so psychology wishes to dispense with the social as the only level on which the meaning and significance of individual experience can be understood. This leads to a view of emotional experience as certainly central to life – of the individual, that is – but the significance of this feeling is seen as essentially organic or biological and as basically innate. Freud is the obvious example of this position where emotion, particularly anxiety, is either the result of undischarged libido, and thus instinctual, or is a physical state of bodily tension produced by stress.[19] The meaning of feeling is almost free of social referents here and, presumably, misery and happiness are in some primary sense 'the same' wherever and whenever they occur, and as indexed by invariant bodily signals.

Pessimism from a psychological perspective is more likely to be a signal of an emotion than to involve an emotion itself. It is likely to act as the marker for the object of a feeling. Psychologists seem to be dealing clearly with feelings of despair, resignation and hopelessness in relation to particular objects, especially nuclear war. Rowe's examination of the consequences of living with nuclear weapons is a powerful and therapeutically practical account of the mechanisms for dealing emotionally and cognitively with not just death but the annihilation of the personal sense of existence. She also describes some of the social conditions for feeling worthless and objective reasons for the current sense of the condition-ality of the future.[20] Lifton has shown the response of the sense of self to the newly realised potential for mass death.[21] There are numbers of studies of the fears and anxieties about nuclear war, particularly among the young.[22] All of these do, in some way, deal with the social conditions of a particular state of mind and the rootedness of despair in the social world rather than in the expressive psyche. That is, the fears are treated as real and not pathological. But the bulk of psychology treats such feelings as expressions of psychological deviance and as an innate disordering of thought and feeling.

An appropriate example of an attempt to locate the social conditions of fear and disappointment within an analysis of the psychological response is seen in Lasch's two recent books and in particular *The Minimal Self*.[23] What are examined here are personal survival strategies at the level of mentalities in the face of increasingly possible disaster from nuclear war and environmental decline. Initially the psychological response to the technological and political situation was a turning inwards of commitment and feeling towards *self*-consciousness and *self*-fulfillment, that is, what Lasch calls 'narcissism'. Then the response is to 'survivalism' as a way of living through and after what is taken to be inevitable disaster. The sheer weight of crisis colonises and dominates the psyche and reproduces itself emotionally and cognitively. It enforces a retreat from a long term commitment to a secure world through political partici-pation. It enters the social state of mind in all its concerns and becomes the mode of experiencing everything – not just the state of the world from which the crisis originates but also the private, personal and domestic worlds. This domination of all thinking by the sense of panic and desperation leads to the loss of ability to discriminate between what are really important issues and the less significant ones. Lasch describes a range of

effects of this state of mind from a vacuous 'global consciousness' which is pathological because it has no boundaries and is
a fantasy[24] to a selfish, anti-democratic form of elitist survival
of the technologically and physically fittest.

These are the social effects of a form of social consciousness,
of a social state of mind which is powerful because of its
individual emotional salience. Lasch tries to link sequentially
the two levels which are conventionally separated in analysis.
Social conditions lead to a mentality which in turn leads to
aggavated social conditions. He also tries to link them within
consciousness itself where social conditions are sustained by
their emotional significance. There are other examples of
attempts to do this in cultural history and the history of
sensibilities. Richard Sennet has tried to describe the life of the
psyche and of personal expression as best seen through
'beliefs' which are 'an activation of the logical cognition of
social life' but where emotion and feeling is seen as less
important.[25]

One of the most helpful discussions of the role of emotion
and feeling in sociological understanding has been provided
recently by Hochschild.[26] She is not concerned with pessimism or even specific emotions so much as the significance
and management of feeling in everyday life and particularly in
the workplace. This is an empirically based study of airline
flight attendants, bill collectors and a general sample of
students, but the empirical research is used, essentially, as
illustration to a set of ideas about how we can usefully conceive
of emotion in the social sciences. Hochschild tries to unite the
organismic psychological model of emotion from Darwin to
Freud, where feeling is treated as a biological phenomenon,
with the 'interactional' sociological model drawn largely from
the work of Erving Goffman. Here social factors do not just
provide the occasion for emotional experience but they actively
shape and craft that experience and its expression. She treats
emotion as one of the senses, as one of the ways through which
we learn about the world. As such to treat emotion as either an
area of residual irrationality and distortion in human experience, or, alternatively, as scientifically hard to conceive or

handle, is in both cases to marginalise it, and is wrong. Emotion is central to life as it is lived, and although she does not explicitly make this point, we could say that this is one of the most profound gaps in our understanding of culture and social interaction.

Hochschild's 'new social theory of emotion' is the exemplar of the unity between sociological and psychological understanding of the social state of mind. Thus what is felt, how it is expressed in action and how this feeling is managed by the subject and others in interaction are all profoundly socially relative. What remains as an absolute must be some biological and invariant set of bodily changes which as yet remain imperfectly labelled.[27] For Hochschild, emotion, as one of the senses, is a signal about how we apprehend our environment. But it is not just a vehicle for information about that environment. It is a *comparison* which relates perceived reality with our prior expectations. It is, thus, connected with (perhaps in the least self-conscious way of all social phenomena, certainly less than cognition) our sense of survival over time. It follows from this that it is a highly relevant dimension of our social experience of social change. Of course this is merely to flag the importance of emotion and to complain about its near invisibility in our discussions of culture, ideology and sensibility. It says nothing about *how* it is to be operationalised. This will be the concern of the next section but at this point it is worth noting that pessimism is an exceptionally appropriate form of social consciousness on which to base the empirical study of such a social conception of emotion.

One final heuristic comparison may help in this discussion. The status of the study of language in sociology may be a model for the study of emotion. Language has come to be a major interest for social science as both the medium of expression and, in some ways, the representation of the substance itself of social phenomena.[28] Its form as a grammar and a phonemic structure can be seen as socially variable but also translatable. It is a system of categories which contains and moulds social reality at the same time as describing it. This is complex and dualistic but it is profoundly constitutive of the social disciplines. As Giddens points out, language is a means of social practice and is also bound up in those social practices. This dualism gives language its complexity. It performs many functions but without doubt is a core form of social activity. So it is with emotion. Feeling is profoundly implicated in our social practice as both a form of representation and as a determining force in its own right.

IMAGE AND THE SOCIAL STATE OF MIND

The foregoing discussion has some clear indications of what can and should be studied as social states of mind and how, for example, we can empirically describe pessimism. I want to suggest the notion of 'image' as an operational and indexical version of the social state of mind which has an attached method of research.

An image is a way of making personal sense of social experience in terms of a movement between past and future. It is a sort of scanning device of society, or part of society, but one which has an emotional dimension which gives it relevance and significance in a private as well as a public context. Social consciousness is a *relation* and not an object, as I have already noted, and image is a *projection* rather than a depiction or representation. In this sense it meshes with Hochschild's understanding of emotion as resting on a comparison of reality with expectations, as a dynamic and relational capacity. This can be contrasted with other conceptions of social consciousness, such as those assumed in most versions of ideology, where it is treated as a set of static assemblages of pre-existing beliefs waiting to be monitored. Here, to exaggerate only slightly, the social state of mind is treated as a more or less coherent set of opinions ready to be polled, or perhaps, at best, as sets of emotionally charged, relatively permanent and fixedly held ideas about specific social objects. These latter operationalisations of social consciousness allow survey work to be undertaken in which stable and coherent patterns of social relations are distilled into indicator or symptom statements which can be used to distinguish simple agreement or disagreement with an externally derived view. They are not, usually, rooted in respondents' immediate social contexts and must necessarily rely, as an artefact of the research tool, on respondents thinking like researchers.[29]

Davis makes the difference between image and opinion clear.[30] His book, *Beyond Class Images*, is within an important research tradition in European sociology which has tried to investigate perceptions of the class structure, usually in relation to the respondent's occupational position or in relation to some theoretically postulated account of class consciousness.[31] Davis reviews the origin and uses of the concept of image as a creative act and an exercise of the imagination, especially visible at times of social crisis; 'image is a bricolage of symbols, concepts and expressions which may be governed by personal experience, hearsay, knowledge, an ideology or (as is most likely) a combination of all four.'[32] As such it may be ambivalent and even contradictory, unlike the social theories of the academic observer. It is not a hard and fast set of fixed views to be triggered or provoked by impersonal survey techniques. Its equivocal nature, however, is not the result of personal incoherence or inability but is informed and moulded by, and is a construction of the society in which the subject lives. The inconsistencies, instabilities, fractures and apparent contradictions are what is significant in image as an indicator of social consciousness.

The earlier work of Willener is suggestive of the use of the imagination itself in constituting the meaning of the image from the subject.[33] It is only a short step from considering the emotional prominence and urgency that image can display. That is, if image is an active, constructive form of understanding the world, it will have to be a felt as well as a thought process. Otherwise it will be just a cognate version of the sociologist's deliberately intellectualised theories.

Some examples might help. Emmison in a recent account of class images of the economy detects inconsistent and contradictory consciousness within groups of managers and shop stewards in Australia.[34] He proposes the idea of 'vocabulary of motives' – first suggested by C. Wright Mills[35] – to help us understand the resources from which image is constructed. Mills suggested that motives were built out of socially available justifications. This availability may be increasingly dominated by the mass media of communication which provides the structured reservoir of what *can* be said by respondents about an issue. By extension we might examine the socially structured availability of emotion, that is, the available and acceptable feelings about issues which provide the emotional dynamic which will allow image to be significant to the subject, or make it impossible to express. A 'vocabulary of feelings' is, presumably, related to social diversity. It is variably connected to images through a tacit agreement on appropriateness, effectiveness and even desirability.

Touraine's work provides yet another example.[36] Social knowledge for Touraine is the understanding of society as a system of action which itself can be conceived as the creation and articulation of values. The image held by social actors is a recognition of these values and is at the same time a participant in their creation. It takes particular shape around the comprehension of alternatives. His study of an anti-nuclear protest group in France tries to show the group producing a counter-model of society and becoming a 'prophetic' movement. The oppositional and counter-factual – or imaginative – character of the group is recorded in his detailed description of the group's discussions, and the striking feature is both the place of feeling in the interactions between group members (they feel deeply and express it) and their conscious perception that *feeling* the anti-nuclear issue was a major part of what gave the issue its significance. Of course this group was an unusually focused one and was ostensibly in existence to deal with images and to persuade and mobilise them. But the account of these activists does illustrate the potential of image as a researchable conception of the social state of mind which could incorporate the emotional dimension of social consciousness.

One of the conventional objections to seeing pessimism as a tenable concept might be that it cannot be characterised sociologically or psychologically, that it is neither an observable characteristic of social groups nor a personality trait. It does seem to have a variety of potential attachments – to feelings and judgments, to a view of time and possibly metaphysics, to particular situations. These may appear to point in different directions, have no clearly defined meanings and generally leave the feeling of imprecision. Additionally pessimism may pose a behavioural dilemma if we view it as synonymous with despair, namely that it is incompatible with continued life, which we conventionally continue to believe requires hope. But it will not go away simply because it is a confusing description of thought for social scientists. It engages too closely with our unhappy feelings and our view of the future. Our behaviour does respond to our thoughts and feelings about what could happen. The overemphasis on the cognitive aspects of thought has left a gap in our understanding of social responses to danger and opportunity. The social state of mind is an amalgam of cognitive and emotional elements which can be assessed through socially situated images. Pessimism is such a social state of mind and could be researched as such potent images, variously expressed and effective.

CHAPTER 3

THE CONCEPT OF PESSIMISM

The concept of pessimism is conspicuous by its absence from social analysis and by its dramatic presence in modern social consciousness. In times as troubled as these the loss of confidence and faith in the future and, more pertinently, the present is manifested as a demoralisation in the public realm, increasingly in the private one, but only obliquely in the social commentary upon each. Sociology conceived and nurtured through two centuries of confident assumption of inevitable progress has found it difficult itself to view the future as probably rather than contingently bleak and has tended to see such assumptions in others as irrational.

Yet pessimism has existed in the background for those two centuries as an available concept with logical, historical and emotional force, and it is possible to see the present period as one of the increasing dominance, initially implicit, now increasingly open, of pessimistic assessments of possible social changes. All social analysis is a form of premonition and the last decade, particularly, has seen anxiety rather than hope dominate anticipation. This is only possible because the conceptual repertoire is already available to permit this sort of change. Sociologists have not suddenly switched from optimism to gloom. They have rather slowly dropped the optimistic assumptions of amelioration, betterment and progressive social construction, which seemed to define their profession, from their manifesto. With a few notable exceptions most theorists have retreated into areas of social commentary which minimise any kind of attempt to describe the future (in fact deliberately not to assume the future is, of course, to adopt a position on the future).[1] Broadly there has been a switch from a concern with the possibilities of long term social change and the potential for social intervention which previously characterised sociology into either an inward-looking preoccupation with theory itself,[2] or, where there is a concern with social as well as sociological issues, a pervasively bleak view of our potential control of events and processes. As a highly generalised and synthetic intellectual approach to the future, sociology is simply the most obvious example of the turn away from optimism and progress. It is an amplification of a more general cultural shift, even though the message is often faint or distorted as it is processed through the regular institutional forms (educational curricula and publications) and is filtered by its inherited intellectual apparatus.

None the less there is a sort of vanguardist role for social science. One of its uses is to detect the social state of mind, to decode the variety of signals and to make sense of them in a number of ways and then to play them back into public debate. It did precisely this during the most energetic periods of social engineering when it both monitored and amplified public and specialised beliefs in social improvement. The same role is available now as a receiver and transmitter of an entirely altered set of understandings of the future.

In this task, of what use is the concept of pessimism? Is it a justifiable decoding of the social signals in modern culture? If it does make sense of important changes in recent social consciousness why is it not more widely revealed? In order to answer these questions it is necessary to examine the background and the provenance of pessimism and optimism and their usages in other discourses, academic and public.

PESSIMISM IN SOCIAL THOUGHT

The words 'pessimism' and 'optimism' have such strong

common-sense, everyday associations that it is startling to understand their recent and specific origins in the eighteenth and nineteenth centuries. So commonplace and mundane is their use, applied routinely to gloomy or to hopeful *temperaments* that we might assume that they refer to universal features of human nature and have always been bandied about in the same way. But two hundred and fifty years (in the case of optimism) is not a long time for the term to exist and this implies that the social circumstances which called it forth and gave it meaning and value can be seen as historically remarkable. The origins of the terms become significant if they can be located in this way. That is, it is the specific introduction of new concepts, reflecting and shaping new ideas, which supports a claim that some concepts are significantly socially relative.[3]

Interestingly optimism occurs before pessimism as a recognised term.[4] It enters the vocabulary after Leibniz' attempts in the early eighteenth century to rationalise the beneficence of the Christian faith and to provide an ethical basis for the practical politics of bringing peace to a Europe damaged by recurrent wars. Pessimism becomes generally accepted only in the nineteenth century.[5] There is an assymetry here, then, which reveals the priority of such sentiments, attributes or qualities as were implied by the two words.

The words codify and express ideas which have been part of the apparatus of social thought since antiquity. These notions in Greek, Roman and early Christian and indeed other religious thought concern what seem to be timeless antinomies – between good and evil, pain and pleasure. The late entry of these ideas as compressed terms, as easily and newly available intellectual currency transmits this universalistic, essentialist or, at any rate, *a prioristic* meaning but connects it first of all to religion, for optimism, and then with the secularist, rationalist, even psychological critique of religious faith with Voltaire and after. But the words refer to the attributes and qualities of the universe, or to mankind as a species. They have no explicitly social connotations but generally refer to metaphysical or spiritual absolutes. This meaning became solidified and the terms quickly marginalised as a consequence. Social thought became analytic, critical and based upon empirical science for its criteria of judgment. Pessimism and optimism were seen as references to those levels – individual temperament or the transcendental – which were irrelevant to serious social discourse for some time.

The origins of pessimism and optimism lie in philosophy. But the terms have meaning in a range of other discourses and can be seen as important themes in artistic and imaginative work where, although not used in a literal or an analytical mode, they are traded upon in clear ways. This use is testament to the power of the ideas.

In academic discourses pessimism and optimism have some currency in biology, philosophy, psychology and the history of ideas apart from the self-consciously social disciplines like sociology and economics. The range of uses is revealing of both the variation in meanings and explanatory significance given the ideas so far. This range can also be viewed as a set of 'levels' of discourse which are, to a degree, connected and interpenetrated.

In biology, and currently in 'socio-biology', there is sometimes an unexplicated assumption of optimism which is used to support the idea of evolutionary advantage. Monod's idea of 'teleonomy', where living organisms are 'endowed with a purpose or project' of which their structure and performance is a manifestation, is the strongest and most controversial version of this.[6] But a belief in a biologically transmitted propensity for adaptation, survival and evolutionary 'success', based in the human genotype and simply made visible in cultural forms, is increasingly widely held by those wishing to situate the sources of social performance in biology.[7] Defined as the propensity to succeed within an environment, such a biological view of optimism is subject to many criticisms from those who are unable to accept such a deterministic position. But it illustrates that an orientation to the future is such a basic part of our social thought that we must project it on to nature itself to give it status and stability.

In academic philosophy, although pessimism is a recurring

theme with respect to morality, the philosophy of feeling and metaphysics, Russell's condemnation of it is still, probably, the typical attitude.

From a scientific point of view optimism and pessimism alike are ojectionable: optimism assumes and attempts to prove that the universe exists to please us, and pessimism that it exists to displease us. . . . The belief in either optimism or pessimism is a matter of temperament, not reason.[8]

If anything, as British academic philosophy has moved steadily in the direction of the philosophy of knowledge and logic and away from the concerns of metaphysics and moral philosophy, such a judgment has been reinforced. But this is quite local and recent. Concerns of eschatology (man's final ends) and perfectibility have been most important in philosophical thought and metaphysical issues still linger on, as they must, even in the secularised social science consciousness. Metaphysical pessimism as expressed by Schopenhauer and Nietzsche[9] or cosmic anguish[10] has been seen as illogical,[11] which is not to say, however, irrelevant or meaningless. The attempt to launder philosophy of the feelings of pessimism and their attachment to essentialist beliefs about human nature is an analogue to sociology's unwillingness to allow feelings and emotion as acceptable data. But ignoring such issues does not make them disappear. It merely displaces their discussion to other discourses.

Eschatology and perfectibilism are relevant concerns, even primary ones, in speculation about the nature of social change and the future. Kermode's understanding of 'the sense of an ending' through fictional literature as a 'deep need' and as endemic to modern consciousness is an extended hint at how deep eschatological concerns can be.[12] He sees it as an existential anxiety projected onto whatever contemporary events present. Even its forms such as 'crisis', 'transition' and 'renovation' may be the givens of all thought. The sources of eschatology in the Jewish and early Christian preoccupations of early philosophy have now become limited to the exegetical projects of modern Western philosophy, though the interest in

Eastern religions and the philosophical implications of mystic-
ism reveals the abiding interest in these topics. In an
intellectually secularised world the religious forms and myths
of eschatologies and cosmogenies are seen as having merely
'symbolic' status, as Gellner suggests.[13] But we still require
'horizons' for our sense of society, an account of beginnings
and endings, however controversial.

Equally basic and nagging is a concern with perfectibility,
which itself rests on some notion of a metaphysically ideal state
of perfection. At its most obvious this may be embodied in a
supreme being or in a post-earthly life. But perfection may also
be seen to rest on improvement in the wordly future through
social action.[14] This latter sense of perfectibility is, plainly, the
basis of the optimistic view of social progress which has under-
written our understanding of society since the Enlightenment. Secular perfectibilism seems not to have faltered until
recently when we have seen a return to the earlier pessimistic
beliefs in original sin which underlay the Augustinian heritage
in Christian societies. The modern versions of original sin may
be expressed as innate economic selfishness, competitiveness,
aggressiveness or whatever but they ground a view of the
future on man's *nature* as essentially evil, even though that evil
may be expressed as self-destructiveness. Modern perfectibilism seems to be increasingly beleaguered and locates itself in
shrinking areas of social action. Now it is in the psychology of
self that we see its most plausible expression, in self-
improvement, self-growth and self-understanding. This is a
very restricted form of optimistic social action compared with
the broad political stage. There the selfish and aggressive
social actor must be faced with a controlling rather than a
permissive set of social regulations, regardless of whether his
overweening character is fixed in individual human nature or
in the necessities of collective action.[15]

The concern with our final ends and with our potential for
limitless improvement can be seen as philosophical issues
which are avoided in philosophy itself and picked up in other
areas. They necessarily make reference to the category of the
metaphysical which, understandably, is seen as an area for

psychological not logical investigation. But these issues of ultimates are not as irrelevant in general social consciousness and in the socially shaped, popular expectations of the future as they seem to have become in the academies. Certainly religion and, probably, popular secular sensibilities trade upon an anticipation of the future which makes reference to these concerns, and perhaps increasingly so as the explicit eschatological and perfectibilist values of the 'new' religions and cults imply.[16] Certainly eschatological 'futurology' – the transcendental, visionary anticipation of a new discontinuous society, whether good or appalling – has long been an identifiable category of imaging the future, and in fictive accounts of utopias and dystopias has sometimes dominated.

Psychology and psychiatry, as I noted in the last chapter, have made some reference to pessimism, and the clinical category of 'depression' necessarily rests on profoundly felt negative judgments of a personal future. But just as sociology has been significantly built on a concern with social problems so psychology, institutionally and academically, rests upon psychopathology and the therapeutic response. Some popular and recent psychological accounts of the 'self' treat *social* pessimism – the judgments made by people about their society rather than just themselves – as the occasion, not for personal despair, but as a diversion into unproductive and, ultimately, destructive channels. Self-absorption and insulation, the popular adoption of psychiatric modes of thought and speech, new forms of 'therapy' and routes to individual 'growth' have been seen as the refusal of a 'mature' or 'healthy' approach to the future caused by its apparent bleakness.[17] A view of the self as located in time as well as space, the sense of the future, of continuation and connection does have psychological as well as cultural implications. However the treatment of pessimism as irrationality rather than as a normal response to social situations probably still dominates. As the data about the behaviour of individuals in extreme and threatening situations comes to seem more relevant to our own condition so we see a coalescence of a sociological view of pessimism, and psychological accounts of despair and disturbance.[18]

The greatest use made of the concept of pessimism has been in the history of ideas where such concepts, produced by intellectuals and professional writers, have been linked to the dominating consciousness of the age. If we adopt a history of ideas approach to pessimism we see interesting variations. There are a few attempts to disinter optimistic and pessimistic views of the future within enormous historical frameworks.[19] But two fairly recent writers have tried to detail the more manageable post-eighteenth century shifts in world view and can be used as examples. Steiner sees the 1789–1850 period as one of tremendous utopian, political vision and optimism which was followed by a reaction of a confused mixture of meliorism and pessimism in the nineteenth century, a combination of economic and technological dynamism and romantic disastrism.[20] The experience of the German concentration camps during World War II he sees as a final destruction of the optimism which began two hundred years previously with the Enlightenment, and the beginning of the 'post-culture' in which we now live. This is marked above all by its pessimism. Steiner's elegant essay attempts to draw on a range of knowledge (including music and painting). Less certain of such a definite extension of pessimism is Wagar's view of the idea of progress since Darwin.[21] Despair and the expectation of catastrophe, he says, have become characteristic this century. Using a wide range of sources, including academic philosophy, *belles lettres*, political and scientific writings (for instance the pessimistic implications of the second law of thermodynamics), he charts a rather more halting course to neo-romantic pessimism since World War I especially via the routes of radical relativism and the increasing awareness of a meaningless cosmos.

These writers exemplify a general synoptic approach emphasising an increasingly pessimistic general culture seen in the context of a more rather than less unified set of intellectual, artistic and scientific representations.

History of ideas approaches are interesting, particularly, because they both exemplify and record the importance of *nostalgia*, the melancholy yearning for a sense of belonging which is often seen as being in the past. The use of images of the past as defences against likely future developments, and the emotional attachment to what is believed to have been the past is somewhat similar to and, perhaps, a component of pessimism. It is often seen, wrongly, as personal and temperamental, whereas it is social in origin and certainly in effect in terms, for instance, of its inspiration of social groups and movements from the romantic socialism of William Morris to factions within today's 'green' movements. To the degree that it does motivate collective social action it is a sign of optimism and may embody clear utopian pretensions. In its vaguest form it becomes mere regret which is usually privatised and inward-turning.

These discourses, which are bodies of professional, academic writing, do refer to pessimism; if not by that name then certainly in its essentials as I have tried to define it. Although it has remained as an unrefined and unpopular term in conventional British academic philosophy, it is too central to social and human experience to be erased from those disciplines which are the reflective commentaries on that experience.

SOCIOLOGY AND PESSIMISM

It is sociology we would expect to have detected and analysed pessimism most clearly among the social sciences. The irony here is that it has displayed pessimism most dramatically and has also been the least reflective about it. This is noteworthy because sociology is certainly the most general, parasitic and synthesising of all the social sciences and at the same time has the most intimate relationship with ordinary language.[22] It has the least possibility, let alone pretension, to detach itself from the common-sense world which is its subject matter and thus it is close to, indeed, part of what it studies. This means that the failure to treat the emotional significance of social consciousness is only part of the general failure to be reflexive and to be a commentator upon itself.

Sociology is necessarily concerned with judgment and with

time. As a form of knowledge it rests on usually implicit evaluative assumptions which resonate with profound cultural and psychological sentiments and feelings.[23] Judgments of the future are a peculiarly powerful type of such evaluations and form a deep layer in nearly all social theorising. This is because, on the one hand, judgment itself is modal to all interaction (the activity of sociology included)[24] and on the other hand time is the environment of all social change. Thus *how* we think is sentiment-relevant and *what* we think is temporally grounded. Pessimism and optimism are concepts in which these substantive and procedural fundamentals fuse.

Pessimism is not just one neglected dimension in understanding some important changes in recent sociology. It is a form of judgment which deeply conditions theory and practice. Evaluative orientations to the future form constitutive judgments which underwrite the form, content and salience of sociology and, by extension, other bodies of formal knowledge. It is worth providing some detail of how sociology has veered from optimism to pessimism during its relatively short existence.

The major founding fathers of sociology were predominantly historically optimistic.[25] The optimistic idea of progress had high status in the eighteenth century French (and Scottish) Enlightenment[26] and later theorists, especially the nineteenth century 'giants' of social science can be seen to be engaged in pursuing this idea rather than questioning it. The early conservatives' tragic view of history as a moral mockery of man's hopes of secular salvation[27] certainly finds an echo in Durkheim's view of 'anomie', Weber's fear of 'rationalisation' and Marx's conception of 'alienation'. Weber always seems to be more pessimistic than most but all of them inherit the progressivist mantle of pre-scientific sociology and use it to clothe, for the first time, precise analyses of modern industrial capitalism. The optimism is evident: Durkheim believes in moral progress concurrent with the division of labour;[28] Weber describes the process of the rationalisation of all spheres of life and at least sees that the tensions between rational routinisation, charisma and democracy can be held in balance.[29] Marx (depending on the choice of texts) provides a dogmatic statement of determinate laws and stages which lead to material and moral progress, or a more tentative utopianism of the post-capitalist romantic and free society.[30]

Early American sociology was similarly optimistic, although for different historical and institutional reasons. In the 1890–1930 period especially, it was immersed in practical social reform and claimed the respectability of a crude but practical foundation in science.[31] The dominance of the 'Chicago School' at the end of this early period with its almost unprecedented intention to deal with social problems gave way to a theoretical renaissance in the USA in the 1920s and after, mainly associated with Parsons and structural-functionalism. Here too the reliance on social equilibrium rests upon optimistic assumptions, especially concerning the necessary fulfillment of functional imperatives.[32] The spin-offs from functionalist fundamentalism into developmentalism posit social differentiation and variation over time in a progressive direction.

Early British sociology shows a belief in the benevolent possibilities of social engineering. According to Hawthorne, sociology at this time is a vehicle for modernists interested in solving the problems brought about by social change.[33] The civic sociology of the 1920s is decidedly Comtist. Hobhouse and Ginsberg's fath in moral progress underwrote the later reform consciousness.

Sociology in all these different contexts shares and amplifies the optimism of its parent culture. Beyond this, and in certain periods (for instance the USA in the 1920s and Britain in the early 1960s) sociology may have been in the vanguard of optimism, focusing and defining the prevailing form of hope. If we can call all these variable strands the foundations of modern British sociology it is plain that optimism dominates.

The retrenchment and movement into pessimism occurs within a relatively short period after 1960. But sociology is not constituted simply intellectually. Like all disciplines it has an institutional existence as well as an ideological one and the relations between the two spheres are one heuristic way of understanding the changes in knowledge. The optimism of sociology's intellectual origins was manifested in the enormous expansion of academic departments in the 1960s and in the appeal of sociology to students, funding organisations, governments and the press. The formal and professional self-consciousness of British sociologists, especially in the 1960s, reflected the combined hopes of a number of popular audiences and clients. This period (still too close to be easily visible) is the high point of optimism in sociology – intellectually and institutionally. The doubts and fears of Marx, Weber and Durkheim were neglected or suppressed as indeed they had been by those writers – though the least so by Weber.[34]

There has been a shift since the 1960s away from this optimistic position. Understanding this movement is complicated by the variety and fragmentation of contemporary sociological theory, a problem not lessened by the crudely oppositional classifications of theory which dominate most discussion of sociological pluralism. But a simple list of the varieties of current sociological theorising reveals a common retreat from earlier optimism.

Critical theory deals with a now pervasive and smothering technical-cognitive interest which dominates all thought. The Hegelian optimism of some early Frankfurt work is increasingly abandoned in favour of a description of the profundity of domination in which optimism is marginalised to an understanding of the real extent of determinism.

Ethnomethodology and the 'constitutive phenomenology of the natural attitude' defines the sociological task as drawing the veil from a social, but deeply uncontrollable, realm of determinism. It avoids the entire issue of social intervention by adopting a neutralist position on the possibility of social change.

Structuralism maps the contours of the social surface by reference to deep, sub-social structures, possibly of the mind, in which some form of naturalistic teleology is assumed. Again determinism is deep and beyond intervention.

Functionalism, which certainly was optimistic in its reliance on stability and progressive differentiation, is less visible in sociology except in the form of an embattled systems theory, and is only residually supported.

Any list of the variety of sociological theory now[35] illustrates the familiar sense that British sociology has retreated into a series of non-social or para-social determinisms which involve a distinct denial of traditional historical optimism and an abandonment of the notion of progress. Weberianism, Durkheimianism and Marxism still compete in the explanation of the forms and importances of the major social divisions in our society. The analytic primacy of production and consumption, the significance of capital, technology and morality, the priority of the economic and so on still exist as rival identifications for many sociologists and these issues do embody inherited optimisms. But they are significantly challenged as the defining form of modern sociology.

In addition to this change in the self-consciously theoretical part of sociology a similar movement can be seen in applied sociology in the form of inputs into state policy-making, planning, social work (in its broadest sense) professional practice, private and public management and administration. As a practical endeavour sociology is in decreasing demand. The only area of conspicuous recent expansion has been in education, especially in secondary schools. This decline, of course, is not so much the result of sociology's own pessimism as of a whole range of economic and ideological changes in its potential audiences. But those forms of theory which fail to support sociology as a practice-oriented discipline have contributed to this. There is a disconnection between theory and practice which has isolated theorists: the hardening into abstract metaphysics or limited empiricism is a tendency which is much more noticeable now than when it was first publicly condemned by Mills .[36]

This fragmentation and schism has enfeebled the intellectual defence against institutional attack.[37] This is a parochial example of the general case that the loss of an optimistic view paralyses purposive action. An exhausted meliorist or critical-rational sociology is weak in comparison with the apparent vigour of those forms of social analysis which remain

apparently optimistic. The notion of a crisis in sociology is a
reflection of changed perceptions and is not attributable to the
nature of sociological thought itself. To repeat, sociology is a
specific illustration of the general collapse of optimism and its
replacement with at least a passive pessimism. In this it
unreflexively and unreflectively echoes changes in general
social thought, but it does so in a manner shaped by its
institutional and academic structure.

The implications of the social science movement into
pessimism are interesting. One of the most obvious is the
difficulty with social engineering or with making constructive
proposals for social reorganisation. This has left social science
intellectuals with only a residual critical role – moaning,
carping or, at best, producing coherent critiques. Intellectuals
have hitherto had substantial influence on technology, production policy and socio-political attitude formation yet this has
not led to 'successful' policies and these areas of knowledge are
seen less and less as 'useful' in a society 'overwhelmed by the
complexity of its own problems and its even more pronounced
internal contradictions'.[38] Thus a major appeal of this kind of
intellectual enterprise – its practical utility – becomes hard to
sustain.

Another appeal is to a more general enlightenment, not of
policy makers, but directed to people's everyday sense of
ignorance. The popularity of the social sciences in mass higher
education was based, in part, on this attraction. The origins of
social science in the late eighteenth century and its consolidation in the nineteenth, that is, its more optimistic period, is
marked by its aping the methods of the physical sciences in the
hope of sharing their prestige and support. Its optimism and
its positivism were linked. The ironic effect of this is that the
social sciences could not become the *human* sciences by this
route because of the deliberate ignoring of the dimension of
feeling and emotion. As Lepenies makes clear, the culture of
reason which banished the culture of feelings only alienated
people all the more from themselves and their environment by
so doing. The result was that alternative forms of social
understanding competed to provide the appropriate philos-

ophy of life in industrial society, especially imaginative literature. When sociology claimed to replace metaphysics and faith it only heightened 'the longing for real beliefs which are to be felt not known'.[39] The literature of feeling, says Lepenies, is a leitmotiv of the secret history of the social sciences. For this reason the popular appeal of sociology is severely qualified by its scientism which is the very reason for its existence. As the claims of social science intellectuals to be superior to literary intellectuals in the field of practical knowledge begin to seem irrelevant,[40] so the same belief in a privileged apprehension to the personal experience of social issues cannot be held either.

The idea of a crisis in social science is so familiar now as to be inert. To add to this diagnosis might seem gratuitous but some of its conditions and consequences with respect to its judgments of the future have been ignored. It is as though social science optimism has been sustained by an increasingly meagre diet of scientistic theories and data and that the fear that alternative nutrition would provoke despair and would certainly weaken the attachment to social engineering has forced it to continue. Alternatives are seen as cranky and not serious.

Yet the fact that there is a crisis of legitimacy, authority and relevance in social science is plain, and to diagnose the crisis as internal to the intellectual form of the discipline seems to be a way of ignoring the changes in general social consciousness and real events.

In a general sense there is a 'crisis of orientation' in all academic disciplines caused by their failure to help solve structural problems.[41] It is aggravated by the fact that in the form of science and technology they have helped to create those difficulties. The belief in a scientific road to progress is severely damaged and, for the first time, there is no prospect of an alternative guiding force, of ways of thinking and modes of action to that failed science. The crisis of particular disciplines can be seen as part of a wider difficulty and as reflecting, in their different ways, the overall collapse in a belief in secular progress. A few social scientists have been saying this for some time[42] but the concepts which could illuminate the issue have remained undeveloped and undiscussed. Instead the displacement of the reasons for, and the feelings of pessimism on to either an area beyond analysis or one treated as an intellectual pathology has sustained a nostalgic assumption of progress in the teeth of despair. This regressive social science will presumably pretend to the possibility of improvement, even of social transfiguration up to the point of social collapse itself.

The idea of pessimism is neither irrelevant nor unfounded. It speaks to a general social condition which is pronounced at the moment. It has a provenance in formal social thought which illustrates its usefulness and it can be operationalised in a way that grasps the felt nature of social expectations.

CHAPTER 4

THE END OF PROGRESS

The idea of progress is so deeply embedded in our social consciousness that to deny it is deeply unsettling. Progress is possibly the most significant single idea for understanding all our judgments about social change in the modern period. It is only in the last twenty or so years that it has been seriously and popularly challenged with a consequential replacement by a variety of forms of future consciousness and of senses of history which are sometimes seen as pathological. The almost ontological status of progress requires an act of intellectual surgery to see it as separable from the understanding of change itself, let alone actually remove it from that understanding. It is difficult to be open about the end of progress. After all what else would be the direction of our lives and those of our children – stasis, regress or nullity? This is an intellectual and an emotional issue, this apparent need for projection with which we clothe our mundane activities, our cultures and our politics, whether this projection is to a religious and other worldly arena or to an observed and experienced society. It is tempting to treat it as such a *need* and thus exempt it from sociological scrutiny with all its relativising tendencies.[1] Certainly the complex meshing of our feelings about things necessarily getting better with our theorising about the forward movement, the serial, sequential and connected development of our society, is so historically remarkable that progress in its modern sense of 'improvement' almost seems to be a psychological datum.[2]

But the idea is becoming emptied of convincing content and what we continue to mouth in all our conversations are rhetorical, even ritual phrases which no longer seriously contain or shape our convictions.

This is what makes the present period a peculiar and interesting time. The public rhetoric of progress, apart from echoing hollowly when struck by the reality of events, is ever more constricted and condensed into a hymn to technology which, in turn, is decreasingly understood by a mass audience except as a form of 'gee-whizzery'. It is difficult to appeal to a secular public with anything more profound, with values, culture or particularly, with history. Although a fully worked out pessimism as a form for comprehending history is the preserve of professional intellectuals, the sheer scale of events over the last few generations – wars, famines, mass torture, attempted genocides[3] – intrudes into mass consciousness as a nagging anxiety which sits uneasily with a political credo of social improvement through technology and through the consumption of goods.

In a substantial survey conducted in the late 1960s and early 1970s Galtung and his colleagues, whilst finding no strong, developed future consciousness, discovered considerable pessimism in industrial societies expressed as a form of 'development fatigue'.[4] The young were the most pessimistic in this survey and this is echoed in more recent researches which reveal a 'post-materialistic' morality combining both pessimism and activism![5] These are both examples of the kind of evidence which supports a view that a publicly expressed belief in progress is difficult now. The implication is that this is new and that this loss of faith in the future marks a change. But in the absence of unambiguous attitude data this remains surmise to be plotted against other kinds of indicator of an earlier optimism.[6]

There is certainly no shyness among social scientists about their loss of faith in progress. When Dunn remarks 'who now, except a complete imbecile, can still expect a guaranteed progress'[7] he expresses a general view, though one which in most writers remains a background assumption rather than a resource or a topic. Few are as open and even fewer, when they do express despair, go beyond rhetoric in order to explain and analyse the basis for these feelings. Certainly *doubt* about progress is analytically acceptable and has probably increased enough to become the dominant attitude among such writers.[8] But the abandonment by social scientists of progress as a subject is itself difficult to contemplate intellectually.

In our personal lives the same difficulty exists. How could we carry on day to day, with all future hoping and planning that this requires, unless we have some, however attenuated, notion of possible progress beyond the very short term. The emotional resistance to the loss of some idea of progress may require that the idea be cloudy and vague and even avoided or denied as an issue in our thought and talk. It is well known that the popular consciousness of progress, unlike the intellec-tualised concepts of academics, is rooted in the material reality of everyday lives. Expressions of optimism about the future are intimately related to the perceived possibilities of achieving desired, local, domestic and personal goals and fulfilling material expectations. Yet even this can now be qualified. It has been suggested that as societies gain freedom from basic material deprivations non-material needs become more impor-tant, needs, for instance, for personal fulfillment or for an increase in the quality of life.[9] New values may inform our idea of progress and not just those of intellectuals but of a generally post-materialistic kind. Thereby our sense of the problems of the future increase in a new way. If such changes are taking place – and the evidence is flimsy[10] – then we would expect our feelings and thoughts about *our* possible progress to be unusually constrained compared with previous generations if only because of the high visibility of exceptionally dangerous events.[11]

This seems fairly recent. The realisation of likely terminality as a background expectancy for most of us dates not from a single event such as the bombing of Hiroshima in 1945 but from the accumulation of problems since then. The accumulation of gloomy prognostications in the 1970s as the economic engines started to falter when deprived of cheap oil, the mounting concern with environmental damage, the realisation of the true costs of economic growth and so on over the last fifteen years have come, by accretion, to weigh heavily on our future consciousness. The least that has resulted is doubt about a progress which was previously entirely (at least popularly) unquestioned. Intellectuals have published their fears for fifty years, not only about the apparent difficulty of science and technology solving our deeply structural problems, but also about the role of that same science in creating them. In the last twenty years this sectional view has spread via the mass media to a much wider audience which, given the scale and intensity of the difficulties, cannot ignore them. Events themselves have fuelled this popular change.

What replaces progress? The deep need for some kind of future orientation cannot be ignored and, after all, progress as the belief in *human* improvement is a quite recent and local form of that assumption. But once experienced as powerfully as in modern Western societies, its substitution is not accomplished without significant consequences.

We can see at least three forms of such a substitution, all in their own ways dangerous in that they refuse to confront the dangers which have inspired them. The first possibility is that fantasy replaces the assumption of progress. That is, we revert to dreams, visions and reveries about the future. Often the term 'utopia' is used to express this orientation, wrongly, as I shall show later. A utopia may include elements of a fantasy as an idealised form of society but it is based upon a view of the possible. A fantasy is by definition impossible. Perhaps the most obvious kind of such fantasy is *nostalgia* which, although its strict meaning is homesickness, has come to represent a regretful longing for the past. The desire that the future repeat, impossibly, a fantasised past which is itself a creation of the present is common.[12] As a mode of thinking it replaces active participation entirely by a blanket condemnation of the present and, by implication, the future in favour of unconstructive complaint which sees the golden age as the high point of civilisation to which we can never return. This mode of coping with the underlying anxiety about the future is avoidance using the past as a tool.

A second substitute for a belief in progress is cynicism.[13] Here the loss of faith in the future is fully accepted and then itself used as the basis for truncating social possibility to short term, sectional advantage. If no progress is possible we must simply set out for what we can get and such selfishness is all that can exist. A good example of this approach is what Williams calls 'Plan X' or 'a new politics of strategic advantage' in our society.[14] This is the fatalistic belief that dangerous developments are unstoppable in our world, that danger and crisis will continue indefinitely and that temporary advantages are all that can be hoped and planned for. It is visible as game playing in the arms race, in the competition for resources and strategic advantage in international relations and in the struggle for governmental power itself. This mode of thinking replaces progress by an absorption in action, in a game which is in constant flux and in which outcomes are limited to only a further stage in the game. Calculation is the kind of activity which is intellectually challenging and in which final effects and morality are never even considered. According to Williams this is the emerging rationality of self-conscious elites and is becoming the common sense of high level politics. It ousts alternative conceptions of the future not least because of its high status location.

A final inadequate alternative to progress lies in making the analysis of the end of progress a substitute for the belief itself. This is a compulsive and academicist pathology where the act of surgery becomes more satisfying than the cure. Much of social science has become fixed in the stance of the fascinated observer where the whole point of the discipline, the end to which it is contributing, be it social reconstruction, general enlightenment or whatever, has become entirely subservient to the act of analysis. For instance simply charting the loss of faith in progress and relating this to social conditions as precisely as possible becomes an end in itself. This is vacuous if it is not accompanied by some attempt to judge and to assess the justification for these beliefs. This is a ticklish point because, after all, this book is in exactly that position – that is making an academic exercise out of something which it is also suggesting is potentially terminally serious. It should be clear that mapping the end of progress can also be directed to a recovery of a new sense of the future if it is not arrested in an involvement with the delights of analysis itself. As a mode of thought it replaces the object of theory – the idea of human betterment – by theorising itself and ultimately becomes entangled in the seductive pleasures of intellectual self-absorption.

These are all avoidances of the issue and thereby failure to confront constructively the task of thinking about the future. The old assumptions about progress are no longer viable but they have decayed in substance only to leave their rhetorical shell behind. We have no alternatives to perform the necessary cognitive and emotional tasks and so the idea of progress operates as a benign and misleading phantom.

THE IMPORTANCE OF THE IDEA OF PROGRESS

The idea of progress is not just a belief about history. It is a regulative moral idea which directs the ethical and intellectual action of an age. It thus has considerable social force. But progress as an idea is like a vehicle the motive power of which has radically altered. So although we can speak of two hundred years of faith in progress this has meant a number of different things over that period.

A brief history of the recent idea of progress should help to introduce this conception of it as interestingly plastic. It should also suggest the unprecedented nature of the present when even such a flexible notion of improvement has difficulty surviving. There are a number of histories of progress available which display the transitions in the meaning of progress as the relief of mankind from bondage to nature through the advance of knowledge.[15] Prefigured by the writings of Voltaire and Montesquieu, powerfully expressed in the work of Turgot, Condorcet, St Simon and, later, Comte, the 'Enlightenment' takes human progress as its organising principle and such a confident idea of progress that sees moral improvement entailed in intellectual expansion. The late eighteenth century saw the founding of a 'science of society' which rested upon a belief in human as well as natural order.[16] The significance of this is that progress required that men know and act, that they engage in social construction rather than just submit to the natural order as some self-balancing machine of which they are merely a part. The optimism inherent in this view of progress should not be exaggerated[17] but the dominant tone was hopeful and this was carried, via the rise of positivism and the faith in science as the cognitive model *par excellence*, into the nineteenth century, into biology, geology and into evolutionism. This latter idea dominated progress and subsumed it in an account of development which has been criticised as a fallacious and pernicious model of social change.[18]

Social evolutionism provided the accepted model for under-standing the future both popularly and scientifically, in biological and social science, especially in the USA and Britain with generally pernicious effects. But it gave a specific metaphysical gloss to a conception of progress. Again it was not uniformly or unequivocally optimistic but in its most powerful social form, as expressed by Herbert Spencer, it was characteristic.[19] Ethical progress and the perfection of human character were seen as an outcome of 'natural' competition. The unity of scientific knowledge – applied through industrialism – and a belief in moral betterment through that very process was the typical form of progress which was inherited by our own century. Although increasingly uncertain and seen as fallible in mass wars, depressions and the visibility of the costs of industrialism, this view has jerkily reasserted itself, since the end of the Victorian period and does so today in various forms such as some of the theses of post-industrialism.[20] But the level of conviction has declined under the impact of a variety of attacks to the point where it is now at least actively embattled and at worst regarded as the grossest form of self-serving ideology. The 1960s were undoubtedly a watershed for the residual belief in evolutionary progress with a realisation, for the first time in the modern period, of the potential terminal point of development. Since then we see resurgent appeals to scientific knowledge and technical expertise as still the guarantors of future progress, though even a feeble evolutionism now seems doubtful as a pattern for the future.

THE SOCIALISATION OF PROGRESS

Such a history of progress is familiar. Its contemporary attachment to science and technology is now implicitly assumed. But within this history we can see that progress as an idea of the shape of history has been very variable.

There are numerous classifications of the content of progress – for instance 'innovational' and non-innovational' progress, scientific and moral progress.[21] What is more revealing than typologies is an indication of the movement of the typical meaning of progress over time. Since the end of the eighteenth century there has been a shift from progress seen in individual terms towards a much more marked social conception, and within this social form from one based on scientific knowledge to one based on social knowledge.

In these terms, progress originally carried the meaning of the increasing release of the individual from constraint to his own or to the world's nature. Such a view characterised religious medieval conceptions and later the conceptions of the Enlightenment. As Nisbet notes, progress at the end of the eighteenth century meant 'freedom' signifying the individual freedom *to*, and whether in this form, or expressed as *happiness*, progress was plainly a condition perceived, assessed and desired for the atomised individual.[22] Once progress is believed to be a quality of knowledge, which is the great contribution of the Enlightenment, it becomes social whatever the form that knowledge might take – natural science method itself, the control of social affairs, the understanding of the causes of economic growth or whatever. I do not want to exaggerate the distinction. Personal potential and social mastery are at least connected in all notions of progress but there has been a tendency for one or the other to dominate and the modern period is one of the increasing 'socialisation' of progress whereby it is society and social arrangements which become the object to be judged as progressive or not.

A fully socialised version of progress would be one which had abandoned the reality of personal fulfillment in favour of a view of society which simply assumed that human happiness was attached to particular social arrangements. In this, technology alone, or economic growth *per se* would be the necessary and sufficient conditions for increasing individual satisfaction. The very resistance to such an idea now and the debate about the quality of life, which does not seem to many people to be simply equated with increases in material goods or consumption, is evidence that a collective notion of progress has not been accepted. None the less we have shifted towards this assumption such that it is impossible to talk about progress except as a set of developments in social conditions from which individual consequences will flow. Moral progress is now seen in some sense as being attached to social progress and, most significantly, the precise character of moral progress is continually altered by social change itself. For instance 'new' moral problems follow on from particular technological changes in weaponry or the control of fertility or the manipulation of information. What is morally progressive in these areas is a novel and newly complex issue.

This change toward a socially dominant progress has within it a detectable movement which could be very broadly described as a transition between two kinds of social knowledge. The paramount position of natural science and its potential for progress through increasing control of the natural world was unquestioned until relatively recently. So progress was marked crudely by an identification with particular disciplines such as physics or biology or, more sophisticatedly, by an identification with scientific method itself.[23] The connection between natural science and material improvement became the paradigm of progress during the nineteenth century and has stayed with us ever since. The whole idea of social advance rested upon a foundation of technical improvement and a faith in the cumulative nature of scientific knowledge.

But we are now in a period which questions the optimistic view of such knowledge, and indeed the linkage between scientific-technical change and moral-political progress. At the very least this implies a dissatisfaction with science as necessarily progressive knowledge. At its most pessimistic it rejects knowledge as such in all its forms as the basis for progress and thereby any secular version of progress itself. But the latter position *is* pessimism in its most extreme modern form and although it is the view proposed in this book that this is a direction we may be travelling in, it is an exaggeration to see it as a destination at which most of us have arrived.

More interestingly the loss of confidence in science as the magisterial form of progressive knowledge can be seen to throw into relief what we might call 'sociological' knowledge or that form of understanding concerned with social organisation, politics, our cultural and economic lives, and even includes social morality and ethics. In part, as already mentioned, issues of social choice and adaptation are made sharper by scientific-technical change. The notion that technology has outstripped our social ability to use or control it gives urgency to a general need for social knowledge to deal with social problems. This, of course, may have technical implications.

A useful example of the turn to social knowledge is that of economic growth. Increases in material well-being, in health and welfare, in democracy and participation and even in equality and justice have been almost unquestionably linked with the process of economic growth since the early development of capitalism and this was expressed notably in the work of Adam Smith.[24] Progress became (and became measurable as) economic growth. The sources of such growth in technical improvement, new machines and new production techniques more significantly than, though not exclusive of, new ways of organising work has been a dominant theme since the advent of capitalist industrialism. Technical rather than social innovation and invention rather than reorganisation are seen to be the prime determinants of economic growth, which itself has become the central, political objective of Western industrial societies.[25] The three part connection between economic growth, technological change and scientific knowledge is a political commonplace at the present time when international competition for such growth has taken the form of a rivalry for control of particular technologies. But it is also a considerably supported anlaytic position, for instance, in the work of Daniel Bell.[26] It is traded upon as an assumption when explaining Britain's industrial decline, for instance in Wiener's thesis that the snobbish and nostalgic aversion of the British Victorian elite from issues of material growth and technical innovation explains the 'English disease'.[27]

We no longer see technology as so central in two ways. First, even though we may accept economic growth as a form of progress or as a necessary foundation to progressive development generally, we may no longer hold science and technology to be the key to that growth. A good example of such scepticism can be seen in Hirsch's important book *Social Limits to Growth* where he provides a most pessimistic account of capitalism in the late 1970s.[28] Briefly, Hirsch identifies, first, the importance of non-material satisfactions in 'positional', zero-sum goods which increase once a certain stage of economic growth is passed; and, second, he notes the underlying importance of social morality, which the capitalist ethic of self-interest cannot provide, and which guarantees the stability of the system. Thus economic growth, for Hirsch, is a social and not a technical process which is potentially in serious difficulty because of its social contradictions. Scientific change and technological innovation alone will be irrelevant to these dilemmas. As Gershuny notes, the logic internal to our social institutions, our material environment and our political choices will determine how we cope with the economic future even now, with the huge wave of technological innovation centring on information technology. That is, even with the current surge of technical invention and scientific change the kind of knowledge needed to protect, let alone extend economic growth is about social organisation, social behaviour and social meaning.

The second way of downplaying technological knowledge is by unseating economic growth itself as progress. The waves of scepticism and doubt since the 1960s about the costs and limits of growth are well known, profound and come from a variety of directions – from economists to the counter-cultural theorists of the 1970s.[29] They have assumed the form, not just of a critique of the importance of economic growth but the foundation for alternative conceptions of social progress. These centre not on materialism or science and technology but on social organisation. Thus new ways of life are concerned with social innovation which may not only reject technological advance but which is oriented, primarily, to the understanding of how people can live in communities without conflict, the dynamics of their social relationships and their values.[30] These alternative conceptions of social well-being and progress turn to forms of knowledge and organised discourses in sociology, psychology, philosophy as well as to versions of biology and physics severely qualified by social accounts of the environment and the natural world.

Of course there has always been an anti-technology tradition of writing which casts progress very much against the scientific stream. But it is only recently that this has become the basis for significant social movements which actively campaign against a scientific conception of progress and, much more generally, an intellectual basis for popular anxieties about the consequences of science. To put it crudely, technology now raises as many fears as hopes for the future.

THE END OF PROGRESS?

The switch away from a science-dominated view of progress is one of the major reasons for increasing pessimism. The most interesting question here is whether this change is a temporary reaction or is a serious transition in the cognitive and emotional basis of our future consciousness. I want to suggest that it is the latter and that this is because we have at last bumped our noses against the limits of controllable physical change. The changes which we now know we need are social ones and we also know that these are difficult and even intractable in a way that previous physical changes were not. In other words the turn toward knowledge of our societies and social selves and away from our physical environments has brought with it the lesson that reliable social planning and control seems impossible. The increasingly sophisticated interrogation of our own history reinforces, not just the existence, but the dominance of the unintended consequences of our intended actions.

The obstinacy and recalcitrance of society compared with nature is a delayed realisation. Partly this is due to a model of social understanding which mimicked the physical sciences and thus echoed their pretensions to control. If we could control nature then, in principle, we could do the same with society using the same methodological approaches. The dripfeed of criticism of this approach to social knowledge expanded to a rushing torrent of near abuse over the last two decades. Alternative notions of a social discipline such as 'hermeneutics' or those which promoted the importance of subjectivity and meaning over structure demonstrated the sheer complexity, variability and ramified nature of social life. If nothing else it gave the impression that systematic and comprehensive social knowledge may not be possible. All that might be achievable may be either a general level of understanding which would certainly be too abstract to permit social engineering, or that knowledge might be local and even personal. To the extent that scientism was abandoned or weakened in sociology so also was the possibility of controlled social change because of the very nature of society. To put it bluntly society is much more complicated than nature.

But the modesty of intention which should follow from such a view of our knowledge is not forthcoming. Indeed the pretensions to control, which all modern societies display when confronted with the profundity of the problems, have led to a new level of difficulties: the solutions create the worst problems. The most obvious examples have been in the exercise of state power in a literally *fantastic* sense such as the Nazis' 'final solution', the Cambodian holocaust and generally those solutions where mass murder was seem as a solution to a problem.[31]But imperfect control when masked by scientistic ignorance provokes unforseen difficulties with its own feed-back effects. This is not, of course, an argument against any interference in society but simply points out that social intervention should be qualified by and organised around the necessary indeterminacy of outcomes. It must be restricted by understanding and ability as well as desire. It is the scale of social intervention rather than its possibility which is qualified by our lack of knowledge.[32]

The social limits to scientific progress are a familiar theme since the late 1960s, a period which was a watershed in our changing notions of progress. The commonplace observation about the 'middle-class radicalism' which was seen to charac-terise the early 'alternative' movements of the 1960s – communitarian, ecological, cultural, anti-technological – is that it was of its time; the final flowering of a period of artificially high consumption and thus temporary, pampered and trivial. Yet this underplays the profundity of the change occurring in the attitudes of the young during that period. There is an impressive enough body of research since the mid-1960s to support the view that what was seen at that time were the surface ripples of a deep transition in modern industrial societies.[33] The weakening power of the whole complex of technologically based, economically oriented, consumption driven conceptions of progress was visible and important long before economic problems 'bit back'.

The oil crisis was a dramatic event which marked but did not cause the change in perceptions. It did however exemplify the dangerous things which appeared to have been happening for some time.

Economic growth slowed down as the post-war boom petered out. The socio-political configuration decayed all over the world as self-undermining contradictions became apparent. Welfare, technology, culture and politics itself appeared to lurch out of a synchronisation with each other which had lasted for twenty five years. There are a number of ways of describing the occasion in the early 1970s of the new anxiety. Although some studies had appeared in the late 1960s[34] the bulk of those concerned with world futures were conducted a decade later. The scene was already set by a renewed technocratic theoretical interest in the future and a growing sense of ecological concern, but these only form the background for an impressive increase in 'futurology' which has been classified in a number of different ways.[35] Some were more dramatic than others. The Forester and Meadows reports and their responses, with their large number of equations and attempts to transcend political issues, captured a great deal of interest and seemed to epitomise the doom-laden quality of such approaches.[36]

This popular Jeremiah approach was effectively criticised by some at the time, as in fact, a form of disguised optimism.[37] The optimistic kernel within the pessimistic shell can be seen in a number of ways: technologically the hope lay with information science and cybernetics in re-rationalising politics; ecologically the hope lay with a political control of resources through re-educated and re-authorised politics; politically the hope lay in a re-communalised relationship between northern and southern hemispheres and in stable deterrence between east and west; economically the hope lay in a re-established international monetary regime and in re-equilibrated competition; culturally the hope lay in the re-establishment of a consensus of more realistic and profound communal values. Each of these sectors produced characteristic predictions of breakdown and most summary accounts concentrate on their pessimism, accepting at face value the apocalypticism which is the form of such accounts.[38] Population increase, mounting relative deprivation, the implications of a positional economy and so on are reflected, as indeed, they should be, as major social problems. But to each warning there is still, at this time, tied the possibility of effective control.[39]

The most pessimistic are concerned precisely with the difficulty of these remedial measures.[40]

So the shift in values and the new scepticism about material progress was not itself dominated by an acute pessimism during the 1970s. But we can see it as the start of a movement towards a later and deeper pessimism. None the less, even at this time, it was a severe questioning of the old ideas of progress and it made plain that the new condition of genuine advance was the *social* control of our material problems and the *cultural* revaluation of our goals. This is a major change in the world views and ethos of a significant section of our society. This disenchantment with the old ideas does not, of itself, generate an alternative conception of progress. It may, alternatively, provoke reactive alternative utopias but these are, in an important sense, reactions to the reaction and are not in any general or consensual way organic constructions of our real prospects. They are more like weapons in an ideological battle, and two in particular – the idea of a spontaneous social order promoted by the 'new right' and pure technologism as a compulsive restatement of an already failed faith – are notably important at the moment.

Is this the end of a faith in progress? The most cautious interpretation is that we are now in a situation of radical doubt and confusion which is strongly tinged by the perception of our past failure. The need for a belief in necessary progress urges that some alternative to a reliance on science and technology be adopted and that the vacuum be filled. The markers of our changing beliefs can be seen in our adoption of a variety of utopias. It is to this that we now turn.

CHAPTER 5

UTOPIAS

There is considerable confusion about the status of utopian thought and writing. Utopias are variously seen as dreams and fantasies, as parodies and pressure releasing satires, as systematic analyses of human nature, as mystic revelations and as hopeful blueprints for social reconstruction. These views are not mutually exclusive and the sheer variety of views may indicate that overall utopias are a significant kind of social consciousness with important functions, distinctive contents and revealing relationships to their social environments and contexts.

The secondary literature on utopias is vast[1] but, surprisingly, it is largely descriptive and, apart from a few notable exceptions,[2] it treats utopian expression as a fascinating genre of writing but one which is, especially lately, not seriously connected with social change.

Yet utopias have considerable significance as visions of realisable futures, as indicators of states of social consciousness and as constructive and integrative forms of popular social analysis. The present period is one in which utopian thought has become severely truncated and compressed into a number of specific channels and in which 'dystopian' thinking has come to dominate.

THE SIGNIFICANCE OF UTOPIAS

Utopias have a very equivocal status as indicators of social consciousness. They are often treated as irrational or illogical because they are speculative. Yet they are not *purely* speculative because this, of course, would be impossible. Utopias use descriptive tendencies, or at least possibilities, in present and past societies and project them into the future. Utopian thought is thus a very *grounded* mode of speculation and is always an extrapolation of a form which already exists or has existed. To dismiss utopianism, as so many have done, as somehow *inherently* unrealistic – purely apart from those who have dismissed it as being dangerous – is peculiarly ignorant.

Utopian thought has at least two remarkably appropriate kinds of importance if we are interested in contemporary judgments of possible futures.

The first is that utopian thinking has considerable emotional salience which is one of the principal reasons why it has been such an extremely popular form of literary social commentary.[3] The most obvious form of such connection with feelings and desires is the utopian's concern with human *happiness* as a social quality which is formally avoided by other modes of social analysis. Happiness is the invisible emotional content in social planning generally and is assumed to follow on from particular social rearrangements without having to be demonstrably connected. Similarly unhappiness is indexed – by rates of behavioural pathology for instance – when social scientists examine social problems. It is the mute, emotional content of social behaviour which social planning cannot rationally address in anything other than an oblique manner.[4] Yet surrogates or proxies for unhappiness – such as alienation – are freely used as if the emotional content which is read back into consciousness from behaviour or attitudes is obvious. The difficulty of talking about unhappiness for sociologists is part of the difficulty of talking about emotions as social phenomena at all. The substance of this happiness, its expression and how it is generated, is enormously varied in utopian writing, but the assumption of such particular forms of happiness is its directing principle: it is an approach to politics directed at the creation of human happiness and this is a way of connecting social arrangements with states of feeling. This, surely, explains why utopias are embarassing to social scientists.

The second significance of utopianism is its explicit orientation to the future and thus, for the observer, its status as secondary evidence about how people think about the future in a particular society. Utopias may be remote or proximate but they are always in a future which is realisable if not immediately probable. They are a major form of popular engagement with the future and supply a set of images and even vocabulary for thinking and talking about the future. The passage into popular consciousness of 'garden cities' or '1984' is some testament to the general importance of utopian writing. Utopias are not just *counterfactuals* – idealised alternatives or reversals of existing arrangements. Modern utopias are extensions into time of some desired or feared characteristics already apparent in societies and as such functions as expectancies with all the political and ideological potency of such motivating visions. Thus a major reason for us to take utopias seriously is their character as an accessible and public means of aspiration by a group in a society and one which embodies a version of time-consciousness which may be, for instance, evolutionary and gradual or which envisages a break or rupture in the sequence of social change. They are a form of envisioning the future which designs what future social conditions *should* look like (or should not) and how they *could* come about.

It is startling that recently explicit attempts to construct plausible utopias have come badly unstuck[5] and that dystopias seem both more popular and more relevant.

FORMS OF UTOPIA

There are a number of ways of classifying utopias. Chronologies are one notable and fascinating way and a number of thorough histories of utopia are available.[6] They demonstrate the longevity of utopia as a significant form of social commentary and the repetition of a number of themes and even forms. It would be redundant to repeat the historical sequence of utopian thought in detail, particularly as this is less important than the contents of such forms. However there are plainly *waves* of such thinking which are remarkable for their changes in content and sometimes in form.

The sequence is broadly from the classical utopias of Plato's *Republic* through those of Christianity's growth, such as Augustine's *The City of God*, of the Renaissance, of the early Enlightenment of Rousseau and Diderot to the late Enlightenment of Condorcet and Godwin, to those utopias of science, technology and production of the nineteenth century much more familiar to modern sensibility.

But the history of utopian thought is not particularly significant from a sociological perspective except insofar as the obvious surges in utopian interest and production are themselves indicators of a particular intensity of social response. The history of ideas perspective, which sees utopianism as a genre of writing with a continuous and self-referential dynamic, is less interesting than a sociological approach which treats the form, function and, most interesting, content of utopias as both speaking to the writers' own social conditions and revealing something to *us* about those social conditions.[7] As Mannheim showed, utopias function in a society in a profoundly political way.[8] The fact that there have been such continuous waves of enthusiasm for utopias is an indicator of the importance of the general form. The precise significance of particular waves of utopianism depends upon our understanding the local social conditions and on the social organisation of the writer and reader in those conditions. These are legitimate historical questions with genuine sociological relevance. Understanding waves of utopian writing is as relevant as understanding the regular patterns of practical utopian experimentation. Both are significant when connected to their social conditions.

Of more immediate relevance is the variation in *form* of utopianising. A commonly used distinction is that between

'classical' and 'modern'. The classical form, exemplified by the
early Christian utopias, is transcendent, metaphysical and is
aimed at the individual rather than society. It is essentially an
announcement of essentials. By contrast the modern utopia is a
manifesto of man's ability to engage in deliberate social
change. It is secular, a critique of existing conditions and an
implicit reform of, or complaint about, social organisation.
The classical utopia is timeless, the modern is a time-oriented
expectancy. It is the modern utopia which is of concern here.

But such a distinction is a very blunt instrument, although it
allows us to bracket off, for the time being, transcendent and
religious visions. Of more immediate relevance is the distinction made by Raymond Williams between the 'systematic' and
the 'heuristic' utopia.[9] A systematic utopia is a detailed
structured programme for change; in fact a plan. The heuristic
utopia, by contrast, is vaguer, less particularistic and is
directed at the provocation of the imagination, of need and,
indeed, of the emotions. Both are forms of what Williams calls
the 'utopian impulse' but there has been a sharp decline in
systematic utopias as the practical experience of them has
increased. Williams believes that utopianism is still a potent
form of future consciousness but that it is now expressed
through a form which is detached from systematic critique or
detailed alternative to the existing social order but which is,
none the less, significant in subjective and private realms of
experience.

This really treats forms as vehicles for the expression of
utopianism. This is sometimes seen as an irrelevant exercise[10]
and it would be pointless if we were only interested in the
classification of utopias for the sake of taxonomy itself. But if
we are concerned with the *impact* of utopias on social change
then the form of their expression may well be important.

For instance, the distinction between fictional and didactic
forms is an important one.[11] Although there has always been a
variety of vehicles for utopian thought – sermons, plans,
designs, tracts, plays, novels, poems, etc – the varying balance
between appeals to the imagination through stories (using
character, plot and narrative) and appeals through direct

instruction or exhortation has a social basis. It has depended upon the social organisation of publishing, the nature of the audience and the wider alterations in the culture and technology of communications. The high points of the didactic utopia have plainly passed and the dominance and increasing variety of fictive forms is seen, notably, in film and more literarily in science fiction and the novel of the future.[12]

Form is important if we are concerned with the social impact of utopias. The days when Edward Bellamy's *Looking Backward* or Ebenezer Howard's *Garden Cities of Tomorrow* could achieve startling popular impact[13] are gone. But enormous numbers of people see films with utopian/dystopian implications.

THE FUNCTIONS OF UTOPIA

Utopias take the form of a literary device. This has led to a degree of condescension about it from social scientists who have distrusted it as a significant form of political discourse.[14] Yet it is precisely this and a great deal more. Utopias have a number of important social and intellectual functions which should lead us to scrutinise their form and contents much more closely. A few writers have dealt with this issue but in general the unsystematic quality of utopias and their huge variety of forms has prompted an unnecessary hauteur. The very quality of utopias as a device, that is as a contrivance, is taken as an inherent unsuitability for analysis, presumably because of its deliberately popular appeal as a fiction. However fictions are simply one form of hypothetical or 'counterfactual' statement about social life and serious social analysis is certainly interested in popular social judgments which must rest upon posing alternatives to what is being judged. Utopias, then, are an important form of political judgment (and sometimes practice) with functions which we should take seriously.

The first function of utopias is what we might call their *provocative* one. Utopias can operate as an active transformative agency which provokes social change and can exert considerable influence on the actual course of events. Far from being some fantasy or aberration of the imagination, which is popularly treated as just an entertaining fable, utopias can become part of the political process itself. Utopias have activated and energised some of the most profound and even cataclysmic political changes in the world such as the Soviet revolution, the German Third Reich, or more distantly the American constitution. Certainly socialism itself, which has had the most fundamental effect on the modern world, was deeply utopian in its theoretical and, later, practical formation.[15] One of the most well known (and idiosyncratic) sociological observers of utopia, Mannheim, made this practical and active conception of utopia central.[16] Unlike 'ideology' which was harmonious with reality, passive and acceptance-oriented utopia aimed to burst the bounds of existing reality. It attempted to achieve a transformation and a particular future. In fact the utopian mentality was one of the most important causes of social change and a major political catalyst. There is some difference between the *direct* effects of particular books or tracts and what Bauman calls the 'activating presence' of utopia in the general culture. It is one of the proposals of this book that the contemporary emptying of *general* utopian concern from popular and elite cultures is very significant and that although we might be able to point to specific utopian proposals which have motivated particular sectional publics there is little salience overall for the transcendent and transformative which utopianising embodies.

The second function of utopias is *evaluative*. It proposes ideals and allocates priority to particular social formations, traits, values, groups and organisations and it compares these ideals with the present. Thus it does not just display *possibilities*, it proposes *desirables* and is a dramatic kind of social criticism. Although the form of such criticism often arouses hostility for reasons that have just been mentioned the substance deserves to be taken seriously. All utopias are commentaries upon the present and its social problems. In the utopian societies proposed, these problems – whether they be of technology, of communality, or identity or of morality – are solved, or in the case of dystopias they have come to dominate. The solutions are themselves evaluations of the present agenda in that they focus on social arrangements which, although familiar only in miniature or as half-baked proposals now, are none the less part of political discussion and are tied to particular competing groups. Utopias are evaluations in two senses then. First as a form they embody the critical attitude to things as they are. Second they support programmes for the future which are already part of the political and cultural competition.

But there is an added dimension to the quality of judgment in utopian thought. This, to take up a theme introduced earlier, is their emotional value and their very direct connection with society as a *felt*, as well as thought-about, phenomenon. Utopias and dystopias are popular and dramatic, not because they are some kind of fictional 'trick' but because they have the ability to emotionally move us. They project our desires as well as our thoughts. There is a kind of yearning for the future – or a fear of it – which is as significant a determinant of our attitudes to precise possibilities as are our calm and logical assessments. The judgments of our own times embedded in utopias are the more powerful because they connect with (and in some cases perhaps help to discharge) anxieties which are deliberately excluded from more formal kinds of political discourse.

In summary, utopias are a unique kind of criticism in that they are freed from the procedural restrictions of the social science research report or the political programme, but they address the same issues, trading upon their emotional salience, using a literary form with popular appeal and hypothesising social improvements which are otherwise seen as impossible.[17]

Finally utopian thought functions as an integrating and constructive form of consideration of the future. Once again by its very form it must go beyond the voicing of discontent or complaint to the positing of an alternative, and for that alternative to be credible it must represent the connection and integration of the elements of the society it proposes. It must demonstrate how things *could fit*. Often the ambition which such holistic accounts betray becomes the object of criticism. For instance a notable recent utopian proposal by Bahro required the redivision of labour, and the complete redefinition of the meaning, in practice, of education and communication.[18] Not surprisingly this has attracted scorn for the very scale of its reinterpretation of the present.[19] But such descriptions of ideals which take the systemic nature of society seriously must necessarily go the whole hog to be convincing, and criticisms for 'unreality' are the price that must be paid. No other form of social criticism has this breadth of vision and very few others have this constructive intent. Indeed one of the most frequent complaints about academic sociology is that it is a form of parasitic criticism which depends upon that which it attacks and which cannot escape institutionally or intellectually from this dilemma. Utopianism is not thus attached or suborned and its primary task is the provision of motivating visions.

Utopianism may be epistemologically suspect, it may be unverifiable and not refutable and it may be drenched in values and oriented to the deliberate manipulation of social change. But it is the most valuable, extensive, popular, politically relevant and – most important of all – inevitable form of systematic speculation about the future that we see.

OBJECTIONS TO UTOPIA

Up to now utopia has been treated as useful and desirable. Plainly this contrasts with conventional views which treat it as a pathological form of thought with dangerous political and psychological implications. The term 'utopian' has become one of mild abuse or at least ridicule and in order to rehabilitate it we should examine and evaluate the principal objections to it.

There are two major attacks on utopia: the philosophical and the practical. While we can scrutinise each separately they function in a connected way in general political discourse

where historical readings of past utopian attempts are inter-
laced with a contempt for speculation as epistemologically
proper.

To take the philosophical objections first it is appropriate to
use Popper's well known hostility to utopianism from a critical
rationalist perspective as central.[20] For Popper, utopianism is
philosophically irrational because it is concerned with ends
and we are unable to be rational about ends. Rationality is a
quality of *how* we approach goals not of the goals themselves.
No reasonable debate about ultimates is possible. The
criticism here is of apriorism and of privileging ideas
themselves over data and experience. There is in this sense
nothing to distinguish utopianism from metaphysics. But if
this position is pursued what then does determine ultimate
ends? Popper's position, as has been pointed out,[21] requires
that only what already exists – everyday life – can determine
ends because only this area is subject to empirical trial and
error. Thus what is privileged here is the existing political
order and reason is biased to that advantage.

Critical rationalism concentrates on *procedural* rationality
with the cost of substantive vacuousness and can never address
what a fair, just or good society could look like, for even
idealising such qualities[22] becomes an empty abstraction. Full
blown utopianism is seen as a dangerous version of the same
mistake in which a 'nowhere' world is made attractive by
appeals beyond rational argument and with 'putschist' possibilities. Plainly utopianism challenges critical rationalist limitations on what kind and degree of social commentary is
desirable. It extends the notion of rationality beyond the
procedural by acknowledging that debate *is* concerned with
ends whether we like it or not. A dissatisfaction with a
Popperian approach does not automatically support a utopian
approach, of course. But once critical rationalism is seen to be
too limited as a social philosophy, utopianism becomes a viable
mode of social thought.

The practical – or perhaps political – objections to utopianism are connected (at the least in that Popper is again
associated with one kind of such objection) but also analytic-

ally distinct. At root such objections rest on the view that utopian thought is absolutist, has inherently totalitarian implications which themselves lead to violence and coercion. Utopian societies are seen as necessarily 'unfree' and this has been the most substantial basis for general criticism.[23] Again Popper is the *locus classicus* of such criticisms. His primary concern is with historicism, the underlying belief that history unfolds along a predetermined path which is discoverable by men, and utopian thought is historicist in the extreme. Utopianists seek to transform society in a direction given by their necessarily abstract and comprehensive vision. They are activists engaged in engineering a future which itself will be static and arrested. Utopianism is a kind of religion in that society is abased before the dominant forces of history.

But most significantly of all, utopianism *necessarily* implies totalitarianism. Force will be required to initiate any utopia, exercised by a strong, centralised minority government – in effect a dictatorship. The use of violence is an entailment of the irrationality of utopian thought itself in that as there is no such possibility as a perfect society, and consequently no possibility of our apprehending such a state, no perfect people from which it could be constructed and no possibility of perfect, spontaneous agreement on it, power – and thus violence – will be used to solve disagreements between utopian planners rather than reason. For Popper, utopias require that some people impose their beliefs on others.[24] This assertion that utopian thought requires authoritarian politics, and is contrary to tolerance and political openness, is common to others[25] who also extend and elaborate the implications of the utopia-is-irrational argument with an account of past omnipotent states. These were often constructed at times of deeply felt re-evaluation of the effects of such states; Popper, after all, wrote against the 'utopianism' of National Socialism and Stalinism.

Yet such a criticism, in effect, condemns the exploration of all social alternatives theoretically.[26] Utopia is merely one category of such systematic speculation which will certainly fall if the general criticism is sustained. But as we have seen the argument from rationalism alone is not strong enough to condemn what is not only an inevitable kind of social thought but one which is no less worthwhile when performed systematically and holistically. Further it is by no means clear that utopianism is as strongly historicist as Popper or his supporters have asserted. Utopianism as a mode of social thought is more varied than is allowed by such a characterisation and includes visions of a future state of society *not* derived from an 'understanding' of the logic of history but from many other sources. These may be as dubious as, but not the same thing as, historicism. Utopianism is discredited by an association with intolerance and coercion which is not convincing and depends upon an alternative which itself depends upon necessarily utopian elements. Popper's own proposals for a world government and Hayek's support for a spontaneous social order have strong utopian elements in them.[27]

These criticisms of utopia are well known as arguments. But they are arguments which are widely practised. A recent example of using utopia as a criticism is seen in Selbourne's grossly pessimistic account of what he takes to be the illusions of the contemporary British Left.[28] He accuses the Left of escaping into the twin utopian fantasies of continuous economic progress and continuously extended political participation which then function as distractions, dependencies and displacements from more pressing and practical issues. For Selbourne the 'demands of peace, the cause of nature, the rights of woman'[29] are unattainable by labour and their pursuit siphons energy away from the principal political battle which concerns the defence of individual human rights from violent coercion. Regardless of whether one can share Selbourne's segregation of issues he provides an instructive example of the fear of utopianism, of the fear of an authoritarianism required to make utopian proposals real, and of the 'unreality' of the content of those proposals when judged as extensions of the present. Above all he displays the despair about the future which follows the abandoning of all utopian projects; because the present is so dangerous, a view of the future as merely a version of the present, without the possibility of radical change, is one of increasing appallingness.[30] He allows that counter-factual 'possible worlds' are necessary for 'human speculation and human action' but are not as necessary as facing the true nature of this one.[31] It is in this unreal and illogical separation of the present and the future that we can see the poverty of anti-utopianism.

THE FADING OF UTOPIAS

This century has seen considerable evidence of attempts to build and to live utopias. By now we have remarkable experience of such attempts at radical transformation. The virtual collapse of *popular* utopianism recently can, in part, be related to the oppressive weight of these apparently failed experiments. It would require considerable innocence to ignore the practical consequences of these utopian formations in all fields, political, cultural and economic. It is increasingly hard to point to new worldly utopias and the most dramatic versions which do qualify – such as varieties of 'post-industrialism', the versions of social order offered by the 'new right' and perhaps that offered by some forms of feminism – are not variants of an overarching optimism but the outgrowths of very specific, local and different social conditions.

It is increasingly easy to see *dystopias* – idealisations of the negative and feared. Such accounts are not new but their predominance is. There is an apparent preponderance of weight, frequency, popularity and impact of dystopian over utopian visions within the usual great variety of forms.

It is a familiar comment that there has been a recent decline in utopian thought.[32] If this is taken to mean *popular* utopianism then it is plainly true. While we can point to limited, specialist and academic utopias there are only a very few broad based utopias with general appeal. Indeed fictional dystopias have soaked up popular enthusiasm for some time now. If we take fiction as indicative of popular enthusiasm many writers have noticed that we live in an age of end-dominated crisis in which expectations of catastrophe at the most extravagant, and a general mood of disenchantment at the most mundane levels characterises our fiction.[33] Fictions of the future are dystopias and we experience only what Steiner calls 'the utopia of the immediate'.[34] This is a startling contrast with the fictive utopias which have dominated the earlier periods of utopian enthusiasm. An obvious recent example of the dystopian turn can be seen in science fiction which is an enormously popular form of writing and which is predominantly dystopian in an increasing range of forms.[35] New science fiction utopias are published but are a conspicuous and eccentric minority in a mode which since the 1920s and 1930s has projected new hells rather than new heavens.

This, of course, is only one kind of indicator but it supports the more general observation on cultural pessimism in this century that we have either experienced a loss of images of the future for the first time or that those images are horrific. New popular utopian prescriptions would be a self conscious novelty – which may explain their popularity when expressed as part of political programmes.

If we can accept that utopianising is fading how do we explain it? I have suggested already that it has been the failure of utopian *practice* that has destroyed faith in utopian thinking. Essentially this refers to the failure of *socialist* utopianism. Marxist socialism has been seen as the utopia of the modern epoch.[36] The romanticism and, indeed, Prometheanism, of Marx's own writings have always made Marxism a plausible candidate for optimism, and we cannot understand the contemporary contempt for utopias without addressing the issues of how socialist practice in the past is understood and the socialist utopian agenda today.

Early socialism in the nineteenth century had strong utopian impulses centring on the social conditions for harmony, co-operation, community, equality and justice which have taken a second place to a concern with the mechanics of gaining power within the socialist parties in capitalist societies. Within the West, claims for socialist success rest only on the contribution of socialism to the formation of the welfare state and that itself is now under attack. The utopian element of socialism is either downplayed by socialists or is seen as dangerous where history does display anything other than its gradualism. The most dramatic test of socialist utopianism has been the experience of its actual practice in the Soviet Union or in China where it is irredeemably tainted with, and condemned by, its totalitarian formation. This historical judgment *is* the force of Popper's criticism of Stalinism rather than of utopianism as such. This is not to say that there is no utopian element left in Marxist socialism but that its historical expression is not a basis for its modern renaissance and as, once again, *a popular* vision it has little credibility based on its track record.

There is an apparent progressive thrust to modern Marxism which seems to be optimistic. But the status of all Marxisms as critiques of existing order ('the counter-culture of capitalism' as Bauman calls it) is not enough to rest a convincing utopian optimism on. The vagueness of contemporary socialist utopias (which indeed in many variants of Marxism reaches near invisibility) is striking. There is a difference between the reformist prescriptions of some versions of Marxism – essentially extensions of an existing system – and the utopian dreams of others. Is a collection of reforms a utopia? What we should be searching for in Marxism should be consonant with its own revolutionary basis.

The most obvious examples of this can be seen not in West European or North American academic Marxism but in Marxism as a doctrine of armed revolution, especially in the Third World. Active revolutionary movements in this sense subsist on clear views of the progress of history and the role of men's agency in a Leninist way. There is a degree of religious fervour, even chiliasm, in such Marxist movements which is shared by militant groups in industrial capitalist societies and who also look forward to a golden age. Action of this highly committed kind must be based on hope which literally fights for the realisation of utopia.

But if we except this field of Marxist political struggle it is hard to see an unequivocal and energising utopia in contemporary Marxism. In many ways this is germane to European Marxism's own modern crisis – it has run out of clearly optimistic ideas; it has been tried and found unsatisfying. The implicit utopias of the elimination of alienation, repression and exploitation in all their forms, the re-centralising of consciousness and the substitution of non-economic goods for the crass materialism of capitalism remain as undetailed and, if anything, more unlikely than in the writings of Marx himself. The most explicit Marxist utopias often seem the most absurd. Visible in the work of Marcuse (or Reich) they are grossly romantic, anarchistic and even infantilely sensate and irrational.

The absence of convincing and motivating Marxist utopias has been an issue recently. In the English Marxist tradition the championing of William Morris by E.P. Thompson as an example of a viable and neglected school of thought is an interesting case.[37] Morris' *New from Nowhere* (1891) is seen as a genuine attempt at the 'education of desire' and as a remedy for the socialist concentration on knowledge and analysis with a view of affective and moral consciousness – the 'other half' of culture. Utopia here is addressed as an issue of sentiments, convictions and even feelings. Morris is important to Thompson for the rarity of his *moral* vision of communism. However this vision remains separate from intellectual formation in Marxist thought and recent attempts to integrate such a utopia, such as Bahro's, remain rare, difficult and hardly popular. Overall the experience of socialism in our time, and the present form of utopianism within Marxism, begin to explain why socialism itself, as the most fertile seedbed for modern utopianism, is now fading in this function. By extension it explains why utopian thought itself declines as its principal source of sustenance no longer attracts.

NEW UTOPIAS

If one of the forms of contemporary pessimism is the loss of utopias – most dramatically from socialism – and in general an unwillingness or inability to image the future, it is important that we qualify this general view by its significant exceptions.

There are at least two politically powerful and popular optimisms with their associated utopias which are part of political discussion at the moment. The social utopias of the 'new right' and of 'post-industrialism' are optimistic visions of the future and have come to absorb much of the dynamism of our residual hope of progress.

The 'new right' is a portmanteau term for a loose collection of writers sharing a dominant view of the fundamental goodness of an unregulated social order. There is no agreed and formalised body of new right thought and it is essentially a practical coalition of a number of distinct positions united as a reactive critique of socialism. But it does have a general set of principles which allows us to discern a distinct utopia and an optimism which functions as a deliberate political instrument.[38] These utopias are essentially those of neo-liberal economics on the one hand and of social authoritarianism on the other. The former, while it is economic in form – based upon a faith in the price signal and the market as the most basic social entities – is also a social doctrine. It holds to the benevolence of individual struggle (for self-enrichment) and the 'creative destruction' of capitalism as a social formation. Basically society is seen as a *natural* order in which satisfactory social institutions arise unintentionally. Interference, conscious design via planning and the 'politicisation' of social provision are all seen as dangerous disruptions of a spontaneous social order. It is this latter notion which provides the main foundation for a neo-liberal utopia which although familiar as an academic position in, for, instance the work of Hayek, has a genuinely popular appeal. This is because, on the one hand, it is reactive to decades of state intervention and thus generates enthusiasm by the strength of the contrast with what has gone before, and, on the other, it trades upon a naturalism, an individualism (almost a biologism) which has always had a common sense appeal. This utopia is felt to be radically remedial and is a reflection of a general distrust of intellectual 'meddling' in a world which is experienced as necessarily complex and confused.

The utopia of social authoritarianism is, in many ways,

contradictory to that of neo-liberalism[39] but co-exists with it as a political programme reactive to 'socialism'. It is concerned with authority, tradition and, perhaps, nationalism which may conflict with economic non-interventionism. But it has a reliance on 'human nature' and 'instinct' in common with neo-liberalism, an evangelical individualism which sits uneasily with a concern for family and nation.

In popular terms the two branches of the new right function more as a duet than a tandem, and likely conflicts remain muted or, at least, non-antagonistic. The pseudo-religiosity of appeals to authority and 'natural' hierarchy are never, in political practice or manifesto, counterposed with the libertarian programmes of *The Omega File*.[40] The utopia which is suggested by the new right programme is very close to that described by Mannheim in 1936[41] as a historical version embedded in the present and expressed openly only as a struggle with other utopias. Part of its popular attraction is that it is a utopia which disavows utopianism and claims the authority of the self-evident rather than the deliberately chosen. In present circumstances contradictory positions unite into a programme for social regeneration, as a novel address to the massive social problems which have worn down predecessor social democratic governments. These problems are redefined as essentially the second order consequences of interference with market mechanisms and new right governments come to power with policies to reverse decades of state intervention. New right proposals appear optimistic because they hold that there are directions yet to be followed which have been long ignored yet, on reflection, this optimism is secured not by the intellectual clarity or historical persuasiveness of its basic ideas but on their directness and appeal as a critique of socialism. None the less there is a battle of ideas as well as political practice going on in which the plausibility and attractivenes of the new right utopia is a major issue.

The utopia of 'post-industrialism' is perhaps a misnomer. A better term would be the *utopia of expertise* for this could include the twin forms in which this vision of the future popularly appears – that of 'technologism' and that of post-industrialism as *post*–technologism. Both are optimistic and persuasive accounts of the future as transformed by *knowledge* or, more precisely, knowledge manipulated and controlled by specialist groups of experts. Both are utopias which assume increasing wealth, economic growth and the expanding capacity of technology (as the expressed form of scientific knowledge) as characteristic of advanced society. Both assume a continuous future, rather than one marked by major disruption, in which man's ingenuity is a guarantee of stability.

Technologism is more than just 'gee whizzery'. It assumes that technological innovation is the most significant *social* aspect to change; that is, it holds to a strong version of technological determinism. Given the almost taken-for-granted status of technological determinism in modern society as, probably, the dominant form of popular historical reasoning as well as the most powerful explanation of current social conditions, the salience of technology-as-utopia should not surprise us. The view that 'the new machine makes the new society' while profoundly wrong is a most plausible common-sense view of the world embedded snugly in modern consciousness at all levels including the utopian. Put most crudely the technological utopia states that social, political and even moral problems of society are susceptible to a technical solution, that progress in all spheres is only guaranteed by technological change and that the society in which we now live is accelerating into new qualitative improvements through technological development. Information technology, robotics, bio-technology and related areas are seen as both now and potentially revolutionising our lives in all areas. There is a sense that the new technology is inevitable anyway and that this mode of social change is a massive and untranscendable determinism. Naturally there is a cultural pessimism about this which many writers have remarked on,[42] but the power of technology to excite enthusiasm about the future is remarkable. We live in a time when not only is technology plainly marketed as the nostrum for all that ails us but also when that same technology is the medium for that marketing and the channel for the distribution of the most affecting utopian images. Two examples may help flesh out the familiar and powerful nature of technology as utopia.

The first is the utopian projection of 'the computer' which is used as a code, generally, for a combination of information technology and 'artificial intelligence'. The notion that computer technology marks a 'revolution' for human society, as far reaching as the industrial revolution, is widely accepted. The computer is seen as penetrating all spheres of our social lives – work, education, entertainment, medicine, domestic organisation – but more than this it is believed that we are at the threshold of the 'Fifth Generation' of computers which will have the potential to dominate core social processes – the creation of wealth, decision making, the nature of work and the creation of knowledge itself.[43] Not only is the computer seen as a potential improvement of the human mind, it is seen as the apotheosis of instrumental reasoning and the climax of the human potential for calculative thought. Thus we are seen as on the verge of some kind of explosion of intellectual control, the detailed potential of which is only dimly perceived but of which the sheer scale is becoming an article of official faith as the 'race' to achieve the Fifth Generation is seen as an international competition.

The second example of technological utopianism is the 'Star Wars', or more precisely the 'Strategic Defense Initiative' proposals of the current administration in the USA. This is essentially to construct an anti-ballistic missile defensive 'shield' over America which will 'render nuclear weapons impotent and obsolete'.[44] The intention was, when the proposal was first introduced in 1983, to produce the complete technological 'fix' to the problem of nuclear war by a combination of laser, particle beam and kinetic energy devices. The subsequent criticisms of this utopian proposal have modified the ambition in a rather fudged way. Thus the hope for complete shielding now seems difficult to defend but the plans are still justified as the most progressive response available to the overarching issue of nuclear warfare. It is technology – even technology in its most untried, unfeasible and fantasised forms – which is promoted as mankind's answer rather than political or social reorganisation.

Both examples display genuinely *popular* utopian thought. They are both widely distributed views which have resonances in social consciousness at all levels from the specialist and analytic to the broad-based and imaginative. They provoke dystopian counter-attacks and specialist, academic criticisms which seem to do little to lessen their mass appeal.

The second form of the utopia of expertise is that implicit in what is often termed 'post-industrialism'. In a significant sense it is also post-technologism in that it is a vision of the future which stresses a new profile of employment and production and a new social structure following on from this. The technology which makes this possible is *assumed* as a means to this social end. It is not stressed as the determinant factor but the social organisation permitted by it is. Post-industrialism proposes an ideology of improvement in the *quality* of life rather than simply increasing wealth.[45]

There are a number of versions of the post-industrial society including an 'alternative' or 'counter-cultural' utopia which suggests a variety of new forms of basic social organisation, consciousness and production which will arise, phoenix-like, from the ashes of the present contradictions. Associated with the work of a mixed bag of deliberate utopians of the 1960s and 1970s such as Illich, Dickson, Schumacher and Roszak this is a very particular version of post-industrialism which requires separate attention.[46] More typical, and certainly powerful, is the work of Bell.[47] He stresses the rise to dominance of the service sector of the economy and of the scientists, technologists, professionals and generally knowledge-based experts who control its development. Society's very needs change as social improvement replaces economic growth as a major social goal and the primacy of theoretical and social-technological knowledge comes to replace the primacy of labour. In summary Bell proposes a utopia in which having, as it were, burst through the technology barrier, we are enabled to move away from economic toward genuinely communal values under the enlightened rationality of a knowledge elite.[48] The significance of this proposal is attested to by the quality and quantity of commentary it has attracted.[49] It combines a recognition of the power of scientific knowledge expressed through technology together with all the residual optimism of the utopia of rationalism first displayed at the end of the eighteenth century. It is the pinnacle of projected instrumental reason but which, unlike the purely technologistic utopia, locates benevolence and improvement with a social group rather than a machine.

These are prominent and, I would suggest, powerful new utopias which project an optimism into public discourse. More, they dominate and colonise optimism. Alternative new utopias, evident in some forms of feminism and within the self-consciously 'alternative' social movements, do not seem to be able to command the broad acceptance, so far, of those of the 'new right' and of 'expertise'. They are both filling the gap left by the decline of socialist utopianism. They are both evolutionary and gradualist in their treatment of transition and they both give a historical privilege to groups separated from traditionally represented class structure.

According to one writer all utopias share four interrelated characteristics, which, to paraphrase, are a belief in progress, a belief in human agency, a faith in calculative rationalism and a belief in a natural harmony of interests.[50] Technologism qualifies but does not deny the second of these features but, apart from this, the two new utopias satisfy all the criteria. But their appearance and political use at this time is more an indication of the poverty of any alternatives than a testament to their inherent plausibility. As utopias, they are beyond judgment. As forms of social consciousness they can be connected to their social locations and their constricted and feeble contents seen in the light of their function for particular groups at this time.

CHAPTER 6

FUTURES

Contemplating the future is unavoidable in our sort of society. Although the last few decades have seen an increase in both professional and popular prediction, as an organised and published activity, it has always been a feature of Western society and, as a secular and technical practice, it has had important political effects at least since the eighteenth century. At the present it seems we have divergent, or possibly just ambiguous, feelings about prediction. We have been battered by forecasts of doom and catastrophe which have proved to have chronically overstated their case and, as a consequence, dulled our receptivity to such messages. At the same time we have found ourselves living through changes, sometimes sharply unexpected and unprepared for, which have provoked a plain need to anticipate what might come next. So, simultaneously, we have a contempt and a desire for a rational conversation about the future. Simply getting it wrong in the past cannot destroy the very mode of thinking about what could happen, though it could modify the form of that thought, its methods, information and the uses to which it is put. In this chapter I want to pursue some of the recent forms of 'futurology', to explain why they have lurched so incoherently between optimism and pessimism and to summarise their overall message which is one of great, if partial, warning.

FORECASTING IN GENERAL

It is the apparent increase in control of our social affairs that has generated our concern with futurology and forecasting.[1] The conviction, inherent in the idea of a social science, that understanding is the parent of manipulation has generated over the last few decades a belief that the future is, within limits, a knowable social entity in the same sense as the present. The future has become, in principle at any rate, *available* as an object of concern, anxiety and even joyful anticipation in a much more dramatic and central way than hitherto. Forecasting displays a huge range of forms from state sponsored think-tanks and international organisations of futurologists to journals devoted entirely to the intricacies of prediction and best selling books of extrapolations.[2]

This degree of concern with the future is quite new. As Kumar has pointed out it seems to begin in the 1960s with the coincidence of a new scepticism about social life in general and social conflict in particular. The specialist concern with the future is, undoubtedly, also a reflection of a more general and popular future consciousness which is anxiety-led as social changes have appeared to become both more unexpected and to happen at a faster rate. The sense of a possible *discontinuous* future was relatively new as decades of unquestioned assumptions of social evolution came to seem unsafe towards the end of the 1950s. Little has happened since then to restore the complacent confidence in a benevolent prospect which would take the pressure off demands to prepare for what might come, or even try to control it.

Contemporary forecasting is varied and highly pluralist in method. There are a number of ways of surveying the range of what can pass as forecasting. We can classify them by the *vector* chosen by the forecaster such as the economy, technology or demography. Here a particular class of variable is chosen as the carrier of the determinant social changes believed to occur. Naturally this involves a prior choice about the nature of social change processes in general, and the relations between such hypostatised variables. Or we can classify forecasters by their methodology. For instance there are those who simply extrapolate existing time series of variables and others who deliberately model the interaction of factors in some sort of feedback-sensitive system, and still others who attempt to identify superordinate shifts or switches in the foundations of social life which will transform society. Examples of this last category might be those forecasters who speak of 'revolutions' – industrial, technological, etc – in social processes.[3]

Methodology is probably a good place to start, as forecasting has lately become fixated upon its techniques as a measure of its value – rather like most other social science knowledge. Over the last two decades the dominant methodology of forecasting has become the systematic model. Simple extrapolations of social trends, while useful for short-run anticipation, have gross problems of maintaining the constancy of the significance of the phenomenon extrapolated over long time series. Ambiguity and the changing social meaning of a variable reduce the reliability of this strategy enormously. The often used example is that of marriage; shifts in marriage and divorce rates are notoriously difficult to use as stable pointers to the future of the condition of the family because what marriage means to the participants has changed startlingly, even over the recent past.[4]

In similar fashion grand theoretical attempts to map seismic shifts in social structure in the manner of the founding fathers of sociology, Marx, and Weber, and to draw with very broad brush strokes the new features of a future society, appear to be too generalised, too academic and unusable by planning agencies. Recent attempts to describe such qualitative changes with overall determinant effects, such as Bell's 'post-industrial society' thesis, and which have created a great deal of discussion, have only been significant insofar as they have been both reinforced and fed by more systematic accounts of social change. They have provided the imagery which more comprehensive and holistic modelling has tried to flesh out.[5]

Increasingly forecasting has come to be dominated by the attempt to model as comprehensive a range of factors as possible, and to measure the interactions between projected changes on a global scale. The initiating developments in this direction were the Club of Rome forecasts in the early 1970s, which were, perhaps, the first convincing quantitative arguments about the potential danger ahead since Malthus. They began a mode of forecasting which has lasted, in spite of our scepticism about just how far such equation-based techniques are reliable. But we can see a number of waves of such futures modelling which have moved between the arithmetic of doom and catastrophe and a revisionist optimism – and perhaps back again.

The first wave was marked by the publication of the Forrester and Meadows reports in the early 1970s.[6] Although the ground had already been made ready by an increase in public debate about the effects of slackening economic growth, about inflation and recession, and also about the early warning signs of ecological danger, the futures debate became loud and urgent following the publication of these two books. For the first time in any serious way they applied computer models to the analysis of global trends. Very broadly the message of Forrester was that industrialisation was producing a shortage of resources, and that apparent technical success would be paid for, within about half a century, with pollution-led collapse. Similarly Meadows *et al.*, with a highly complex system model using a larger number of equations, outlined the exponential cost of pollution control at present rates of technological exploitation combined with the mounting instability of the system caused by population increase. Both books, which achieved very wide readerships and considerable discussion were essentially neo-Malthusian warnings that population expansion and continued industrialisation would lead to ecological disaster and massive starvation because of the finite nature of natural resources. The pessimism in these forecasts was stark: unless something was done within *decades* the world economy would collapse before the end of the century and this was with the deliberate assumption that 'exogeneous' catastrophes, such as war, did not interfere.

These reports set the tone for the whole burgeoning debate

on global futures. They were holistic and global in scope, they used increasingly complex and ambitious computer simulations and interdisciplinary research teams, and they broadcast a highly pessimistic message. A further 'generation' of models followed within two years, the most publicised of which was Mesarovic and Pestel's[7] and which like Meadows' report was supported by the Club of Rome.[8] They were much less concerned about the finitude of global resources, and much more optimistic about likely population-limitation policies. Their pessimism resided in the increasing disparity between rich and poor countries and the political conflicts which this will nurture. For them there is a major and profound crisis of development, of which the oil and food crises are simply early warnings. But the Malthusianism here is much more muted and higher global economic growth rates are assumed. What should be said about these latter reports is that they are still pessimistic in their overall forecasts in spite of a shift in overall emphasis from natural resources and the environment to what is really international relations.

The reaction to these pessimistic forecasts was in the main aimed at their techniques and methodologies. Thus their alarmism was seen as unacceptable, not because there was a convincing alternative reading of the same data, but simply because the original reading had technical problems. This is significant because what we see is a message of gloom and doom which is then qualified rather than contradicted or replaced, and this has been the pattern of reactions to pessimistic forecasting ever since. So, for instance, Rothschild is unhappy with the accounts because they repeat the well-known difficulties of the Malthusianism which motivates them, namely that limits are seen as inherently natural rather than social, and the latter are much less easily determined.[9] Similarly a contemporary major response criticised the Forrester and Meadows volumes for employing a methodology which, although its techniques may look more impressive, is essentially no different from earlier, provenly innaccurate ones.[10]

Scepticism about the danger is not the same as an alternative argument. There are few robust defenses for the prospects for the world which try actively to combat these gloomy founding proposals in the debate about the future. One example might be Beckerman's faith in the social and economic feedback mechanisms which he believed would prevent disaster.[11] This belief in the inherent responsiveness of the market is constantly echoed by apologists for the status quo in their defense of the adequacy of existing institutions[12] and, sometimes, this is attached to a criticism of alarmist accounts for the poverty of their data.[13] But these *are* replies. They are not optimistic forecasts which have been generated by events and by original readings of the information available. They are part of a rearguard action to reduce the prevailing anxiety of 'futurology'. As some recent commentators have noted, even allowing for the technical and professional problems in modelling futures, the fundamental questions posed by the original studies remain.[14] There are limits to both population and capital growth which are controlled by feedback processes which themselves may operate on a very long time scale.

Since the mid-1970s some of those very unexpected conditions which had provoked the new concern with forecasting had themselves changed. The oil crisis had declined, energy problems in general became less dramatic, technology enhanced productivity and many of the other dominating concerns about natural resources, food and population did not disappear but were, at least, relegated to a less obvious position in favour of the immediate concerns of the mounting recession, inflation and unemployment in the industrialised societies. The anxiety about the medium- to long-term future was crowded out by the concern with immediate issues. This led to a brief pause in the stream of forecasting by global modelling. Research into particular sectors, of course, continued and data was collected. But the next wave of explicitly holistic forecasting surged in 1980.

The Global 2000 *Report to the President*[15] was a lineal descendant of the Forrester, Meadows, Mesarovic and Pestel researches a few years earlier, and explicitly drew upon the modelling expertise developed at that time. It was prepared for the US federal government and so achieved massive public exposure through the state public relations machine. *Global 2000* raised, once again, in its three volumes, the spectre of overcrowding, pollution and political disruption on a world scale and used trend data to repeat and, indeed, amplify the highly pessimistic anticipation of food shortages, declining living standards and resource depletion. The key assumption in the report was that the rate of productivity increase per person would decline and hence real poverty would increase. This assumption informed all other sectoral projections, especially those concerned with energy and food prices and availabilities.

Just as this report re-echoed the warning of earlier forecasts so the responses to it were essentially a replay of previous qualifications, attacking the methodology, the analytic assumptions and in some cases even the provenance of the research. However one voluminous set of criticisms did try to go further and present an alternative and optimistic vision of the future, as well as trying to rubbish the report itself. The compendium organised by Simon and Kahn[16] used very long time series and huge aggregations of data to suggest that Global 2000's predictions were plain wrong, and that in the very long term constructive human responses are visible to *all* problems – provided individual incentives and the power of markets were not interfered with. Their assumption, which can be seen to balance Global 2000's assumption about declining productivity, is that a resilient economic and social system can be relied on together with native human ingenuity to overcome all problems short of 'unforseeable catastrophe such as nuclear war, or total social breakdown.'[17]

So, after charting these waves of informed and modelled gloom, together with the reactions to them, what general conclusions can be drawn from forecasting over the last few decades?

THE IMPLICATIONS OF RECENT FORECASTING

There are four main lessons to be learned from the recent history of forecasting. These do not lead collectively towards the acceptance or rejection of the levels of pessimism or optimism implied in the major modelling exercises. They qualify the confidence we can have in any such project, but they do so in highly illuminating ways.

The first lesson is about *how* forecasts can be constructed, that is, about the methodology of future studies. The first point to note is one that has been already raised, that of the usefulness of complex simulations, involving computer techniques, to model interactions between variables. All the important forecasts, as we have seen, have used this approach rather than simple extrapolation or general 'scenario' description. Interestingly those well-known forecasts which have used such a methodology have been both optimistic and generally on the political right, such as those of the late Herman Kahn and the Hudson Institute.[18] The scenario approach involves outlining possible hypothetical futures by a selective use of trend projection, and thus makes less claim to 'scientific' probity. Large and expensive models such as the Mesarovic and Pestel 'WIM' (World Integration Model) with its thousands of equations and expensive investment required simply to keep the data base current have, partly because of their investment value and bureaucratic location, considerable prestige, which may be quite independent of their actual usefulness. The public relations effect of such presentations may well exceed their accuracy, as indeed the last decade has demonstrated and as a number of commentators have noted.[19] The problems of such models are essentially analytic rather than computational. That is, how does any model allow for 'unknowable' variables, which are usually political and cultural ones, and which have turned out to be most important in the real turn of events?

This brings us to the second lesson to be drawn which concerns the ability of forecasters to model social phenomena with any degree of confidence. This is a well-known general issue which stresses both the centrality of social behaviour and institutions in determining the outcome of physical systems, and the impossibility of treating them as if they were physical variables.[20] The increasing sophistication of futures modellers with respect to data collection, and the interaction between sectors, cannot be reflected in their ability to build in the behaviour of social systems because of the prime unavoidable intellectual difficulty – the unmeasurability of social and political systems. For instance, the effect of public opinion about nuclear power, or the behaviour of energy-producing cartels like OPEC, is crucial in determining outcomes. Yet no amount of data collection will allow forecasters to predict these variables. In this sense 'paper and pencil' approaches to probable futures, which are explicit about assumptions concerning social behaviour, are just as appropriate and useful as anything else.

This point cannot be stressed too highly. There is a fundamental and completely irremediable problem in the description of the social world in a realistic way. What has happened with a great deal of modelling is that social phenomena have been treated as if they were unproblematically encoded in the changes in the physical systems themselves. Long time series measuring the performance of some physical sector, such as food production and distribution, or the level of real incomes, is treated as *of itself* displaying the outcomes of social behaviour and therefore no more need be said. Purely apart from the fact that the very choice of indicators which will make any sense of the physical systems is a social and political choice (and this alone is enough to condemn the practice as purely 'technical'), the assumption that technical systems *embody* social systems is illogical and, as we can see from the plainly innacurate predictions which have been made, inadequate. In other words there is a whole realm of information which is needed to make sense of the past behaviour of what we think of as 'natural' phenomena which cannot be treated as equivalent to, or commensurable with those phenomena, but which none the less remains vital to the whole enterprise. It is not the case that social, political and cultural variables have somehow been left out of the forecasts and that they could be inserted. It is that such aspects *cannot* be built in and must remain as genuine imponderables. Thus all that the projection of physical and technical developments can do is to show us the limits and constraints within which social choices remain to be made. The limits to food production and distribution and the exploitation of natural resources are, in some way, made finite by the potential of the earth itself. But what those limits are and how they are approached is a social matter which is in no way implied by those physical resources. There is no 'logic' of exploitation within the character of those resources (or rather only an extremely permissive one). The pattern of their use is socially determined, and this is both historically variable and 'open' for the future. The importance of social factors in most systems modelling is arrested at a recognition of the difference between the potential and the possible reforms which could be made and the routine 'get out' clause about the overall conjectural nature of predictions which is conventionally made.

One of the rare examples of a forecaster who does take social variables very seriously is Robert Heilbroner and who as a result is exceptionally pessimistic.[21] Heilbroner makes the focus of his work the social institutions which will be necessary to prevent catastrophe arising from the massive and increasing gap between the conditions in rich and poor countries. He says that totalitarianism, of a kind not hitherto experienced, will be the only alternative to complete anarchy. Thus the 'cure' itself will engender a major social and political tragedy which is none the less marginally better than the complete breakdown consequent on present conditions. Heilbroner foregrounds politics and social institutions in his projections, but he does not try to model these social factors in any quasi-technical way as past trends. He assumes the past operation of social institutions which have brought us to this condition and treats it as a foregone fact. It is the behaviour of the same social variables in the future which is the determinant factor to which we must pay attention. But Heilbroner is comparatively unusual among significant forecasters both for his sociological focus and the depth of his pessimism. Most treat the projection of physical aspects of social life as somehow perfectly 'obvious' and unaffected by social factors such as organised power, the functioning of bureaucracies and changes in the cultural significance of particular aspects of national life.

The third conclusion to be drawn from forecasting over the last few decades concerns the links between forecasts and *interests*. None of the forecasts examined earlier have been produced in some neutral, purely intellectual context and, indeed, such a context is impossible. Forecasts are constructed *for* organised interests which already have some stake in protecting their position. Forecasting is intimately connected with the use and even the gaining of power by states and agencies which serve those states, directly and indirectly. The general issue is once again familiar, namely that knowledge is produced for a purpose. Forecasting knowledge is simply a very obvious version of that general case. The sheer scale and expense of futures modelling requires that the research organisations involved be political actors. The Club of Rome which was responsible for the sponsoring of the Forrester, Meadows and Mesarovic and Pestel reports, was an international association of businessmen, politicians and academics explicitly concerned to address the capitalist world's political elite. *Global 2000* was produced at the request of the President of the USA. International conferences which have produced both futures research, and, perhaps, more important, the agendas for research to be contracted out to other agencies, have all laboured under the pre-existing political alliances and conflicts – essentially North versus South and East versus West – which are the conditions under which all international activity must exist. Truly disinterested forecasting has been unlikely and those futures writers who are apparently unconnected with particular agencies are anyway engaged in a debate which has been essentially set by those agencies. So when Heilbroner, or Ehrlich or Kahn or Simon write, they do so in the context of an already formed debate in which they must take positions.

Markets and elections are the determining background cycles of futures research.[22] Gloomy warnings or calming denials have both been constructed to preserve a world political order and its social formations in times when turmoil threatened from a variety of political disruptions of that order. Thus Rothschild remarked early on in the debate that the early Club of Rome forecasts were intended to remotivate capitalism and were an attempt at the moral regeneration of the present system via corporate planning, new information technology and de-polluted energy.[23] Similarly the blatant pro-Americanism of Kahn's and latterly Simon's works is clearly produced as a weapon in the cold war with the Soviet Union.[24] More recent forecasts of 'crisis' cannot avoid responding to what has already been said (and not said) from this direction and in reply by the left.[25]

In a very profound sense, then, futures research is an extension of the present. It determines the 'relevant' facts to be examined it tries to create an image of a likely future which can be used *now*, and it reinforces the existing profile of control over the distribution of resources and of passiveness and powerlessness. The questions of *whose* future and of warnings to *whom* in contemporary forecasting are highly relevant. Attempts to address genuine alternatives, rather than just gather information to reinforce control, are rare.[26]

This all rather vitiates forecasting as *practical* knowledge. It is certainly usable but is plainly irrelevant to the kinds of activity needed to construct a secure future. Extrapolations, projections and all the statistical modes appropriate to them, have neglected whole classes of information, which we have very loosely called 'social' data, and which are basic to genuine social reform. Thus there is a functional coincidence between methodology, the avoidance of politico-social parameters and the power interests which direct futures research. The most significant effect of this is to make it impossible to generate alternative cultural goals ahead of the imperatives which are constantly declared as determinant of the future.[27] Economic and technological factors are, at root, treated as the motors of social change the speed and direction of which are under the control of the industrialised West. The possible future is by this means colonised by the local present and the crises, manifested in material forms as environmental degradation and resource depletion, are left unconnected to both current political positions and possible cultural alternatives.

The final conclusion concerns the self-fulfilling nature of forecasting. What one writer calls 'the petty unfolding of technological possibilities'[28] exercises a peculiar constraint over constructive thought. Such is the extensiveness and the penetration of the debate about futures over the last fifteen or so years that what I have tried to show as the very inadequate term of the argument none the less dominate the general public images of possible futures. One way of understanding this is as the squashing of the imagination of the future, and one writer who was predominantly concerned with this was Fred Polak.[29] He proposed that consciousness of the future was at the heart of how we order our universe and that failures of the imagination lead to endless projections of present trends. In this way expectations – particularly of disaster – become self-fulfilling. It is essential that we have imaginatively available the 'other' to provide the motivation to transcend this backwards-pulling tendency and Polak saw this as the function of eschatology and the religious vision. Since the Enlightenment this element has disappeared from future consciousness and he feared that the capacity to, literally, *imagine* the future was a lost cultural trait which foreclosed the possibility of avoiding the fulfillment of our own disastrous expectations.

The role of despair and the immobilism which it leads to is well recognised by futurologists of the 'right'. The role of an ideology of progress, which we might well wish to see as a faith or, at least, a motivation, is seen as important by, for instance, Kahn and Simon.[30] Therefore it becomes important to encourage such a belief on secular and technical grounds and this leads to a sort of smug ethnocentrism, and even nationalism, which, ironically, contradicts the very possibility of transcending our difficulties. Indeed it just replays the difficulties and crises transformed into 'transitions' and 'temporary pressures'; the past becomes evidence of the 'historical certainty' or mankind's ability to overcome all difficulties.

There is a sense, which is more than rhetorical, in which we are 'pulled' by the future as well as 'pushed' by the past. This was the significance of utopias described in the last chapter. It is also the importance of forecasting in that such studies of the future define the possibilities. Therefore a constricted, manipulated and sectional view of the future permits a set of policies which respond only to those perceptions and their underlying interests. Through this ignorance and partiality they build out the possibilities of avoidance and genuine changes of direction. Particular power relationships which lie at the root of the world's difficulties are thus reinforced in material fact and reified in our beliefs and, even further, live on to create their own nemesis.

TIME AND CONTROL

Much of what we can usefully say about studying the future depends upon our understanding of time. The purely instrumental attitude to time, upon which the sort of forecasting described above rests, is a parallel to a similarly manipulative orientation to space or place which underwrites an imperial and colonial mentality. The approach to the future in which understanding is subordinated to control is similar to a geography or a social anthropology which must serve conquest of the subject before all else. The implication of all this is that just as such an approach has led to a near terminal exploitation of part of the globe so it may lead to a destruction of the future. These comparisons of the social significance of time and space should not be overstretched just to make a rhetorical flourish[31] but there is an important link between knowledge and political control in all spheres, including the future.

Time is the least intellectually accessible feature of our social world. It is not problematic for us in our everyday lives, and our common-sense acceptance of its variety of forms – the life span, calendar time, the repetitiveness of seasons – makes philosophical attempts to objectify it difficult and seemingly unnecessary.[32] This means that there is little analysis of time to which we can turn as a resource for treating the future as an object of study. Time is both familiarly 'obvious' and complex simultaneously. Its meaning is culturally specific, and this implies for us that 'the future' has a changing meaning which is susceptible to control and manipulation, and also that it should be opened up to sceptical appraisal.

The most obvious place to start is with the future as an expectation embedded in the present and the past, that is with the future as part of some sequence which has a power to influence events *now*. In this sense the *idea* of the future *is* the future in action through planning and organising. The status of particular images of the future, such as are publicised through forecasting, is partly due to their connection with what *has* happened or *is* happening. In other words our theories of social change, which are simply attempts to justify particular narrative sequences as universal, assume, or try to prove, a connectivity between times as residing in something *beyond* time – such as 'nature' itself.

For instance evolutionist approaches to social change, which view the future as unfoldings of a potential which is visible now, make all sorts of assumptions about the immanence, directionality and continuity of social organisation or behaviour. These have largely obliterated alternative assumptions about the discontinuity or 'caesurial' possibilities of social change which are a lot less comforting but which, certainly at the moment, need discussion.[33] Evolutionist assumptions are probably so deeply fixed in our views of history and change that they have become 'meta-theories' and to dislodge them by comparing them with notions of violent disruption, or even of the 'end' of time, seems wilfully, and not usefully, provocative. Theories of social change are attempts to control the future, intellectually, by giving it 'shape' and significance in terms of contemporary interests. Alternative images, and particularly utopias, can be rival readings of the same sequence or they can reflect radical ruptures with that view of process. But if they are the latter they call into question common views of time as particular connections of institutions and thereby threaten, at least cognitively, the process of 'social reproduction' whereby power and control are monopolised over time. The maintenance of power over time (rather than space) is dependent upon creating a view of the future as *necessarily* continuous with the present.

The common view of the future as in some way part of a sequence, or even of an episode, may be tragically misleading but it is, perhaps, unavoidable. The alternative to seeing the future as an outgrowth of the present (and thus a version of it) or as a repetition of what has already been experienced is to see it as *un*determined and completely open. This may be more frightening than even a repressive but known prospect. There is an emotional as well as cognitive basis to treating the most familiar form of futureness, namely the cycle of our organismic lives, as the template for all time. In this pattern the death of our bodies is only part of the continuation of the species. We accept the inevitability of our own deaths in a way which, it has been suggested,[34] we could not that of the death of humankind itself. There is no available model or metaphor to use for the final end of all things and for the stopping of human time, particularly since the decline of an other worldly destination beyond death in which a heaven or paradise gave meaning to the transition of death. When the Black Death killed about one third of the population of Europe in the middle of the fourteenth century and when it was commonly thought 'this is the end of the world', people could at least attribute divine purpose within a shared theological framework to the terrible events.[35] The prospect of a nuclear war resulting in the destruction of humankind, which is a relatively novel version of a possible future, has no transcendental context to guarantee some version of continuity.

For the first time we are faced with time as a common problem. A popular view of the future which, at least, sees the possibility of the end of all things, has had its assumptions about time made difficult. The very medium which we use to embody the future becomes insecure. Those writers who have puzzled over the possible meanings of time provide some materials to help. Most have been concerned with what we might call 'levels' of time. Here time is seen as a *container* of information and as a coded form of knowledge which allocates significance.[36] Thus time 'contains' data at the level of the person (a life-span with stages of growth and decline), of the society (conventional event-dated history of 'civilisations') and of those social structures which span societies (modes of production and entire epochal forms such as feudalism or capitalism). There is a plurality of times with varying 'shapes', uses and relevances. A choice of time level is made according to purpose. Thus the millennial anxiety which preceded the year 1000 AD[37] and which is now evident again is a response to social tensions which indirectly select a calendric focus. Understanding the significance of this 'political numerology' (other examples are '1984' and the biblical date of Armageddon) is one way of decoding a particular social form of time.

The kind of forecasting we have become used to fixes certain levels of time as the reliable horizon of the future.[38] In this way the interests which determine our forecasting, and the methodologies through which they are filtered, come to stabilise and limit how far ahead we think we *can* contemplate. Thus there is an important sense in which our very awareness of the shape of time, as of space, is politically and socially constrained. The future has become, like the official versions of history, *possessed* by particular groups who manipulate it to their advantage. Making the future a deliberate issue for ourselves requires a considerable act of scepticism.

THE FUTURE NOW

There are two significant conclusions to be drawn from this review of forecasting. First, that limited and corrupted as the futures research is, we cannot ignore it. Second, that we need to examine very different areas of our social experience than have been seen as relevant in that research, both to understand what has happened and, more importantly, to reconstruct a *practical* attitude to the future.

We live in a time of peculiar portentousness. For twenty years the weight of those portents has been pessimistic. There must be a mutually reinforcing relationship between the *sense* of foreboding which has been remarked on for so long[39] and the knowledge produced by forecasts over roughly the same period. However we cannot ignore the overall peculiarity of the present. There seems little question that it is not just that we are newly aware of potential dangers but that these dangers are themselves unprecedented. Although the word 'crisis' has been indiscriminately used and has become a vernacular banality its meaning as 'a time of acute danger and difficulty' and as 'a decision point'[40] does have point today in a way that it did not have before both the widespread practical knowledge of nuclear fission and our understanding of the long-term dangers of applying that knowledge. What is new is the scale and extent of potential danger with respect to our natural environment, our population and our very means of existence together with our simultaneous awareness, indeed self-consciousness about it. The least this may mean to us is that what I would regard as a crisis is treated as a time of 'transition' to some new and benevolent phase.[41] But more generally it is difficult to construct a benign prospect. The data themselves do not help us to decide between transition and end, but what is startling is that the data point towards the *possibility* of the end for the first time. Future research demonstrates above all else that we are now in a position of great *risk*. This is the root condition of contemporary pessimism – the secular belief in the new possibility of destroying or damaging ourselves.

This is not the historicism complained of in the last chapter where a belief in 'laws' of social change led, self-fulfillingly, to the deliberate closing down of alternatives. But it is a consideration of a direction which both social processes and events are taking, and which to ignore by concentrating on the short-term and the local would, in Polak's words, be 'auto-destructive' and 'a nihilistic diversion'.[42]

I have pointed to the partiality of forecasting data and its concentration on tehnical and material factors. The 'missing' information is essential both to any attempt to reconstruct an understanding of how we got into the present difficulty and to practical measures to divert it. The level of abstraction of the futures debate has been determined by the needs of the political and planning agencies which have controlled it. But, as Williams says, 'In intellectual analysis it is often forgotten that the most widespread and most practical thinking about the future is rooted in human and local continuities.'[43] Such primary impulses, and indeed feelings, which are located in a sense of time dominated by the life spans of our children and grandchildren, and in the places where we actually live and spend our lives, are the architecture of our social consciousness of the future. Utopian projections can engage with such impulses much more profoundly than can political programmes or economic plans and scenarios. The possibility of genuine social change requires that we address these primary needs and that is precisely why the self-consciously 'alternative' social movements and their concern with the practical reform of 'ways of life' have been attractive to so many people.[44] They address issues of communality and sharedness and equilibrium without exploitation which are the shadow problems of recent forecasts of doom. Part of our general sense of foreboding stems, I suggest, from a clouded awareness that these issues are not addressed at all by governments but at the same time the way that they are addressed by the 'alternative' movements seems impractical and parasitic. Our pessimistic feelings about the future are at the same time provoked and blocked.

CHAPTER 7

THE MAIN DANGER: NUCLEAR WAR

The sheer number of dangers which surround us is a condition of our present anxiety. But the increasing awareness of the mass of threats and their apparent resistance to solution is itself misleading. It is not the variety of insoluble problems which should cause our pessimism but the *nature* of those problems. Popular opinion is nourished by news values with their emphasis on novelty rather than educational values and a concentration on inquiry.[1] This has had the effect of destroying the distinctions between genuinely threatening processes and events and those which have only come to seem so because of the manner of their announcement. When everything is seen as a 'crisis' the discrimination of real danger becomes a problem in itself, and particular threats, which deserve our undivided attention, are submerged within the gloom-inducing mass of apparent social issues.

The general feeling may be of a 'swamp' of social problems in which the personal and the political are muddled and are shiftingly interconnected, or it may be of an ever-stretching set of concentric 'zones' of difficulty with the self at the centre. Whatever symbolic form the current pessimism and doubt may take – assuming that there is such a degree of reflection connected to emotions – an ordering of issues needs to take place if the anxiety is to be channelled into effective action. Otherwise energy is dissipated in addressing false or minor issues, or the sense of an inescapable morass of problems leads to apathy and paralysis. The rhetoric of crisis has become 'normalised' to such a degree that the very language applicable to extreme problems is routinely used to apply to everyday difficulties and mundane irritations to peace of mind: an obvious example of this inflation of language leading to its loss of power when really needed is 'survival', as Lasch notes.[2] Here a term applicable to issues of death and the destruction of the conditions of life is cavalierly applied to the marketing of anxiety about everything from sexual relationships to career planning.

Beyond this perverse and exploited feeling of surrounding peril there are genuine dangers which are fundamental, supervening and transcendant. They are the core threats to the very survival of humankind as a biological and as a social form of life. They are newly visible to us as the most profound conditions of human destruction and they are, ironically and tragically, crowded out of their rational position at the centre of our fears by concerns which are, by comparison, utterly trivial. The popular consciousness of danger thus often misses and mistakes its cause.

The questions of genuine survival concern the nuclear arms race and our treatment of the natural environment. These two issues, and particularly the first, are hazards which are new, and thus cannot be seen as cultural figments merely replaying old worries which we can relativise away. They are also potentially terminal for social life as we recognise it. Further, we have reached a point where, not only have we created these threats but we have enough self-knowledge to know that we have done so. This is a very peculiar and novel position to be in. For the very first time societies have organised their own demise, have remarked upon this fact and have, none the less, done nothing to remedy the danger. It is not just that there is a gap between specialist and popular conceptions of danger; between the *Weltschmerz* of a decadent public and the state-classified panics of scientists who have lost control of their creations. Indeed, were this true then there would be grounds for the kind of residual optimism evident when H.G. Wells talked of human history being a race between education and catastrophe: education would be the answer. The ignorance and diversion of attention is, however, as evident among those who should know as among those who need not, for it is the participation of those who are best placed to see the threat in the continuance of it which makes our position most dangerous. But disagreement among experts has one important positive effect to be set alongside their failure to disassociate themselves from the political structures which underwrite weapons development and the abuse of nature. It creates a space in which ordinary citizens and lay people can make up their own minds.[3]

The risk of a nuclear war and the terminal insults now offered to the natural environment are dangers of startling contemporary seriousness which fully justify current pessimism. They are not examples of the range of material grounds for current forebodings – they *are* the grounds. Fashionable anxiety is absorbed, however, by issues completely secondary to the real problems. Trying to divert this discontent on to targets which deserve it is absurd. Reconnecting pessimism with its real justifications, although it may appear to be little more than a Jeremiad, is all that remains.

It was remarked by Walter Benjamin in the 1930s that a 'left melancholy' of contemplative self-absorption was common among those who retreated from socialist politics.[4] This was a sort of inward turning of consciousness upon itself and there is a parallel risk of this today, as both the intractibility of the problems and the failure of protest in the very face of their enormity combine and reinforce the appearance of inexorability. It is in the light of this situation, where the problems appear to outdistance all available intellectual models and all plausible forms of protest, that the true grounds for pessimism lie.

THE NUCLEAR ARMS RACE

The problem of nuclear weapons has been with us for forty years. It is certainly the case that the bombing of Hiroshima and Nagasaki caused a lurch towards danger of a hitherto unknown kind. But it is only in the last decade that we have seen the maturing of the fullest danger nascent in those early events. We are now in a position to understand the full profundity of the threat we all face from the potential use of nuclear weaponry because we are living in (and hopefully through) a period of major destabilisation of the control of such weaponry, and this instability arises, as we are now able to see, from the interaction of a number of only apparently separate instabilities in technology, social organisation and geo-politics.

So much has been written about nuclear war, and to such little effect, that not only is it difficult to frame a distinctly sociological contribution, but there seems little audience for one. The 'party of peace' and the 'party of war', hawks and doves, military strategists and unilateral disarmers seem to feed off each other in a communal monologue which gets louder and more demonstrative but less and less devoted to seeking a practical way forward. So virtually any contribution to the debate is probably speaking to the converted or insulting the committed. However new data about the effects of nuclear detonations and new understandings of the system in which weapons are developed and used require some mention, even if the conclusions drawn are increasingly gloomy. The intuitive sense that the threat of nuclear war is appalling and the serious discourse, which either tries to modify this with notions of 'limited' nuclear war-fighting or massages the fear with simple horror stories, are too far apart. The contribution of social scientists, with the honourable exception of psychologists, has not been impressive.[5] Natural scientists and physicians have been eloquent in the description of the nature and consequences of the weaponry,[6] and political scientists have contributed to debates about the relationship between international diplomacy and military positioning. There is a developing sociology of war[7] but apart from a few exceptional contributions on the political economy of the current arms race, it is not marked by a concern with the outstanding issue of our era.

What can be said by sociologists in general must remain parasitical upon the data made available elsewhere and all that is presented here is an attempt to describe the novelty of the present situation by surveying some of the recently published summary accounts. Very broadly these concern new evidence about the effects of a nuclear exchange (at levels much more modest than previously planned for), about the importance of the changing weapons technology (including the technical control and command systems for these weapons) and about the multiplying 'temptations' to engage in a first strike (including the political and strategic doctrines which mis-understand the weaponry).

The most powerful statements in the nuclear war debate have been about the effects of nuclear explosions. Books like Schell's *The Fate of the Earth* and films and television programmes like *War Game* and *Threads* have reached considerable audiences, and the passion generated by the appalling prospect of the nuclear aftermath has done much to galvanise the peace movement in the 1980s. The overriding concern with the consequences of such a war is surely correct. How else are we to orient ourselves to the issue except in terms of its likely effects? Yet within this essential literature of horror there lies a trap which is understandable yet limiting to the development of arguments. There is a perverse quality to the catalogue of destructive consequences which can either simply repel by the nature of the excess which must be described, or which can fascinate by the sheer incantation of those excesses. In part this is a problem of communication. A bald list of effects expressed in a clear and non-technical way but which relies on scientific evidence[8] will have a small popular audience. A heartfelt and deliberately rhetorical account such as Schell's can both numb the sensibilities and revolt, or it can encourage a 'celebration' of the effects as the issue itself. I do not want to belittle these works which have done so much to raise the very issue of nuclear war as a genuinely public one recently. But I do want to point to the problem of effective communication about nuclear warfare which, if we dwell on effects and popularise the horror of what could happen, tends to paralyse a popular analysis of all other issues. In a sense a concern with the aftermath seems to make the 'foremath' redundant. There are psychological issues here about the ability of people to understand the enormity of the consequences and to be able to continue to respond emotionally in a constructive way to which I will return. But it may be the case that once likely nuclear effects are stated – as they have been – nothing else can be said except to repeat the message. This may be why little is now being published for popular consumption about this issue and why what is being produced tries to regain the shock effect by setting the horror in a new form such as a novel or even a cartoon or play.[9] If the discussion of the effects of nuclear war has diminishing marginal returns, what can be said about effects and to whom?

The realisation, from 1983, of the possibility of a 'nuclear winter' poses this issue most clearly. Essentially this resulted from investigations, carried out since 1982, into the climatic effects of various levels of nuclear weapon detonation.[10] The conclusions, which have not been seriously challenged after reviews of the evidence by national governments, are that very modest numbers of warheads exploding are likely to cause irreversible climatic and biological effects over the whole globe. The threshold is about 500–2,000 nuclear warheads which is about 10 per cent of total warheads held, on a very conservative estimate.[11] The effects are to increase cold, dark, ultra-violet light, radiation and fire-created poisons to such a degree as to threaten the extinction of the species at most and seriously assault the biological support systems of all societies and the eco-system of the globe at least. In other words nuclear war is a Doomsday Machine above a threshold which our armouries reached in the 1950s, and these climatic effects will ensue *on us all* regardless of our initial position as aggressor, victim or 'neutral'. These are genuinely novel conclusions which truly justify the term 'omnicide' as applied to nuclear war. We now know that we risk much more than we previously thought and the stakes are accordingly raised to ultimate levels.

This research, producing results which are so plausibly

awful, has been ignored, played down and generally marginalised by nuclear policy makers. Nuclear winter renders much strategic positioning and policy-making completely redundant: concepts such as first-strike, limited nuclear war, counter-force targeting and, notably, civil defence which were incoherent politically even if they had any residual military and ideological meaning, can now be seen to be completely meaningless. *Any* nuclear detonation above the threshold severely threatens the world. Nuclear weapons are unusable at any current level of possession and, as a deterrent threat, they lose their plausibility accordingly. The policy implications are all in the direction of reducing the nuclear stockpile to below threshold levels. The official response so far from the USA has been to use the 'Strategic Defence Initiative' proposals for ballistic missile defence (so called 'Star Wars') to shift the nuclear explosions likely in any exchange beyond earth's atmosphere. Apart from the technical fantasy that this embodies, it signifies the official refusal to listen to the argument in a rational way. It translates what is being said into terms which fit with the mentality which is locked into the old view of the effects of nuclear war. They are not really listening because it is too dissonant with what they believe *independently of the evidence*.

If political leaders, as distinct from the general public, are a separate audience for research on the effects of nuclear war they are less amenable to education. If the general public becomes revolted or hooked on the horror of the aftermath and cannot move beyond this except to bid, where moved, for fantasy solutions such as complete disarmament,[12] policy makers are simply deaf or incurably 'addicted' to nuclear weapons for psychological as well as economic and political reasons.

The nuclear winter discoveries are the most dramatic example of the inability of our understanding of the consequences to deter us from creating their conditions. But research on the full effects of nuclear war, even before this, was received with astounding insouciance by the political elite, at least in the West. The British Home Office preparations for civil defence are simply the most well-known example of appalling ignorance combined with obdurate refusal to listen to the evidence on the real scale of nuclear attack effects.[13] The real meaning of what national 'survival' would mean following a nuclear exchange was the subject of an impressive report prepared for a US Congressional Committee in 1979.[14] This made clear that simple 'physical' accounts of damage and best-case versions of medical consequences grossly underestimated the problem. What most accounts, inspired by civil defence or strategic planning authorities, ignored were the interactive and synergistic effects of one form of damage on another. Biological and physical resource survival ignored the whole area, additionally, of social values institutions, social and economic relations essential to make population and productive capacity meaningful. Admittedly there has been a serious failure by social scientists to describe the specifically *social* consequences of nuclear war, and fictive accounts have been rather more impressive.[15] The evidence available to the authorities on the real nature of a nuclear 'national injury' has not only been greater than acknowledged but has been culpably ignored as relevant.

THE DIMENSIONS OF THE DANGER OF NUCLEAR WAR

Research into the potential effects of the use of nuclear weapons is much more extensive than that into the social effects of their presence in our societies. Nuclear weapons cannot be disinvented or ignored: international antagonism will not disappear. These are the two inescapable facts of political life which provide the setting for the changing meaning of nuclear weaponry. They are the context within which changes in the level of danger occur. We can grasp the dimensions of this changing danger by separating the details of these two obdurate circumstances into sectors or dimensions. This provides a convenient way of describing a system of interactive components which is increasingly complex and ramified and potentially unstable. Thus we can begin to grasp the deep penetration of these weapons into the social and economic substance of our societies and their increasing functional domination of social change. Thompson's well-known description of 'exterminism' as a social formation visible at all levels of society, is a paradigm of this kind of description, though with overtones of technological determinism.[16] It is possible to see three interconnected social dimensions of the current arms race: the technology of the weapons themselves, the social and economic organisation of rearmament and the geo-political environment of superpower rivalry.

Some writers, such as Zuckerman, have treated weapons design as an independant variable in maintaining the momentum of the arms race.[17] This view stresses that ideas for new weapons stem from scientists pursuing technical problems within their laboratories, rather than from the military, and the descriptions which have been published of the role of precise groups of scientists and particular laboratories provide plausible narratives of armaments developments.[18] The allocation of the primary responsibility to scientists is difficult as a retrospective account and a useful current position, not least because of the enormous secrecy which surrounds the issue. Plainly the involvement of scientists and weapons technologists is exceptionally important, and whether this role in creating instruments of death is seen as due to the 'moral neutrality', and hence innocence, of science as a unique cognitive enterprise, or whether as stemming from the inherent violence of the masculine motivation of most involved scientists,[19] is an interesting issue. In terms of location scientists are crucial. Whether they are, as it were, out of control or, rather, whether there is an intellectual momentum to technological developments which always has weaponry implications and which cannot be shaped by political direction is a much wider matter than usually considered in this area.[20] Certainly some recent material suggests a degree of naivety and social ignorance, even childishness, among key weapons researchers which is chilling.[21] However, whatever the position we adopt, about the technologists, we should at least be clear about the basic importance of current changes in the devices which they produce, for, regardless of their source, the weapons themselves and their control systems are a primary source of current instability.

It may be helpful if we divide the technology into weapons with particular destructive potentials and the controlling mechanisms which allow them to be used or to cease being used. Most people are aware of the increasing sophistication of nuclear weapons in terms of their extended and variable lethality, the precision of their targeting and the increasing sophistication of their own protection from immobilisation. Delivery systems by land, submarine and aircraft based vehicles and the extension both up to enormously powerful strategic weapons and down to battlefield, 'tactical' nuclear mines, shells and short range rockets has become increasingly sophisticated through weapons research and development. But undoubtedly the most startling example of the power of science as an armourer is in ballistic missile defence, the attempt to render 'nuclear weapons impotent and obsolete'[22] by science itself creating an ultimate techological umbrella to shield the world. Regardless of whether such a proposal is strategically desirable or not, SDI, at least as originally proposed, is the ultimate expression of faith in science as the core of nuclear defence. The retreat from the original absurd proposition of 1983, for complete civilian protection, into something more modest in intention (if still absurd in all senses), betrays a slight bruising of that faith in the face of what is technically possible.

SDI, like all 'improvements' in weapons technology, but much more than anything experienced so far, destabilises whatever pattern of deterrence has been reached up to that point. It is difficult to point to a change in weapons configuration which actually increases mutual security because the science is applied to escaping and even, as in SDI, transcending the existing technology. The logic of weapons development is to penetrate the putative enemy's defenses which, in pre-nuclear military terms, is rational because in those circumstances such new weapons could actually be used. Nuclear weapons are different in kind to all previous forms in that they can have no military use. They can only be used to threaten. Any technical development which seems to prevent the threat from remaining mutual and which seems to qualify one side's ability to retaliate is an invitation to strike first before it can be operationalised. Weapons development *always* increases the threat of nuclear war even when its rhetoric claims it as a peacemaker.

As dramatic as developments in the weapons themselves are, the character of modern control and communication systems to activate these weapons is even more alarming, if less well publicised. However over the last few years several well researched accounts have been published which describe the character of the control systems and some of their potential performance in a likely strategic crisis.[23] The communication networks in the USA, whereby the President must consult and decide on the use of the American arsenal and the actual mechanisms of response once a warning of any kind is received, are terrifying in their likely fallibility. Dependant upon electrical and electronic relays and often using computers designed in the 1960s to cope with data of much less complexity and scale than is the case with modern weapons, the communication networks are simply likely to fail. There is a tragic irony in the technological effort that has gone into the 'modernisation' of the weapons themselves which throws into relief the puny status which has been given to the mechanisms for avoiding a faulty or misguided decision to fire a weapon. In a sense the system is primed to fire and not to prevent firing or to cease fire. It is predicated on the necessity of making a first strike rather than a retaliatory decision and is 'tight' rather than 'loose' coupled to the weapons, which means a very sensitive, alert and even possibly premature response mechanism. The emphasis on C3I (command, control, communications and intelligence), which the last few US administrations have promoted, has not been to make the system sensitive and discriminatory or to cope with the electronic chaos that will result from a war, but has been to make the function of response-striking more enduring. It is probably impossible, anyway, to have faith in *any* conceivable communications system surviving in a nuclear environment.

The shrinking time available to a leader to decide whether or not to retaliate, once he is informed of an incoming attack, is horrendous. According to Frei it is now of the order of three to eight minutes for intermediate range ballistic missiles such as SS–20's and Pershing–11's,[24] The implication of this character of the new weapons is that tight coupling will become automatic via a launch on warning (LOW) basis, or by predelegation of the decision to launch to military commanders who, as in the case of submarines, may become cut off under early battlefield conditions.

A combination of unjustified faith in the discriminatory potential of control mechanisms combined with an increasing tendency to make commands an automatic part of those systems and build out political judgment, however abbreviated, is an unjustifiedly neglected dimension of danger. Both the 'hardware' of the weapon systems themselves and the 'software' of their techniques of management are changing in independently and cumulatively unstable ways. The scientists and technologists responsible for designing these instabilities are, in fact, engaged in tinkering with what they see as discrete and separate technical issues, but which in reality cumulate to an enormously complex and unstable system which could be uncontrollable in any reasonable meaning of that term.

If the technology of the weaponry is the first dimension of danger, the second is the social organisation of rearmament, or how societies economically and politically manage their weapons procurement. The basic point to be made here is that there is a momentum to rearmament and to the increasing expenditure on war-preparedness which is also out of control. At an international level there is an 'arms race' based on an action-reaction pattern by the USSR and the USA but with the former essentially following the USA's initiative in terms of technology. The important issue is to understand how arms are resourced and developed in the West and how they have come to be a commercial and political tail which wags the national dog. Kaldor put the issue succinctly when she described our arsenal as backward-looking and remote from military or economic reality, as 'baroque' and explainable only as the response to the competitive dynamic of commercial armourers and the conservatism of the armed forces.[25]

The expenditure of resources on armaments by a state, together with the political and cultural justifications of that expenditure, are an indicator of the priority of armament as a social process. It is not just the economic importance accorded to weapons development which is notable but the organisational formation and protection of that function. The shorthand way of speaking of this is to refer to the 'military industrial complex' or the 'iron triangle' or even the 'military-industrial-technological-labour-academic-managerial-political complex'![26] All refer to the pervasiveness and centrality of armaments production in Western capitalist societies and particularly recently to, not just its parasitic effects upon other forms of production and development, but its increasing dominance within advanced industrial economies.

Growth rates in military expenditure have varied over time and average growth rates over the last thirty years of about 3 per cent per year reveal very little.[27] More significant are national military expenditures, and particularly military research and development expenditures, as a proportion of national products, or relative to other categories of national spending. The process of developing, making and distributing arms embodies scarce scientific, technical and capital resources which are now the principal mechanism of state-encouraged national change. Spending in this area represents opportunities foregone in other sectors though, of course, it can be argued that such expenditure spins off development into these other areas. The science and capital intensity of weapons development is so great that the military sector has come to dominate, via state promotion, and through the agency of a relatively small number of military equipment contractors, some significant part of the direction taken by civil technology. The most pertinent current example of this process is the use of 'Star Wars' research promotion, particularly since the more fantasy elements of the original programme were played down after early 1985, as the research and development platform for developing particular new technologies. No longer seen as a leak-proof shield from nuclear rockets it can now be used as the political launch pad to justify enormous expenditure on advanced computers, lasers, optical electronics, particle-energy beams and the development of new materials.[28] These are now accepted as among the 'leading edge' technologies and as they absorb increasing proportions of investment resources they crowd out, not just alternative research programmes (for instance into alternative energy sources or conservation or new transport forms), but the very image of such alternatives as possible trajectories for 'proper' science. Thus our societies become shaped, in ways more profound than the simply economic, by the demands of a weapons establishment which becomes progressively more resistant to control.

The most obvious consequence of this process is the difficulty of controlling the arms race. Although the overt pressure for this derives from geo-political antagonism, the substance of this race, and the precise direction it takes, are a relatively independant outcome of the social forms of arms production. This latter recreates itself in the geo-political arena through the need for the superpowers to match each other's weaponry for strategic reasons. Thus SDI research by NATO members will require comparable efforts by the Soviet Union, and ultimately space itself will become completely militarised. The independence of this process, operating at these various mutually determinant levels, is startling: it is out of control. Any proposal to freeze arms developments, let alone cut existing armouries, faces the deeply entrenched economic and ideological interests of the society which has converted a substantial part of itself over to war-preparedness. The mass and the momentum achieved by this institutional change, which is matched in this, if not in its political character, by the USSR, is the truly pessimistic face of 'exterminism'.

We are a society that is preparing for war. We are devoting an increasingly significant proportion of our resources to the creation of weapons which cannot be used, but which are redundant as threats simply because they are unusable. This war-preparation is not explainable by geo-politics but they do provide the most immediate conditions of social instability which makes our military readiness almost incontinent. When we have turned over our science to the service of an unfightable war and turned our scientists' backs on nearly everything else,[29] we have declared as a national priority an obsession with the paradox of deterrence which current strategic doctrines increasingly tempt us to ignore. The third dimension of danger lies in the temptations to ignore the nature of the weaponry's effects and believe that military posturing can lead to political security.

The international political setting for potential nuclear war is the rivalry between the superpowers and the division of the rest of the world into a more or less stable set of subjects. We must assume that this will not change in substance, but that the reliability and stability of control over, particularly the less developed world, will remain labile, contentious and will provide the major grounds for dispute between the USA and the USSR. Similarly we must assume that in such a split world, disputes over influence in one area will always be linked by the ability to respond by destabilising another region (the process of 'horizontal escalation'). Both sides declare their primary motive to be to maintain stability and that the other side's is to increase influence. Such basic motors to foreign policy are, anyway, inscrutable and cannot be reliably assumed to be the sources of foreign policy and military strategy. If this basic rivalry is unalterable, and there is no prospect for 'world government' or a general agreement to disarm, it is within this that we must look for doctrines and policies which aim to use military strength to increase political security. It is here that the most profound ignorance occurs, in that political leaders have come to believe that modern nuclear weapons have some political use, and have proceeded from this point to engage in policy-making which is itself most profoundly de-stabilising.

The change in the West from a nuclear weapons policy

based upon mutually assured destruction (MAD) to one which, in a variety of ways, emphasises that a nuclear war may be limitable, winnable, fightable or in any way prosecutable, is the most seriously disruptive characteristic of strategic policy now, particularly since the publication of the 'nuclear winter' findings. These are doctrines which operate as 'temptations' to engage in a nuclear war and thus ignore the one essential fact about our contemporary armouries; that however sophisticated they may be, they are, in reality, unusable.[30] They derive from a number of sources but all share one feature – their ignorance of the true nature of nuclear weapons. Without describing a history of Western nuclear doctrine in order to detect the sources of present positions,[31] it is useful to briefly describe the most current nuclear temptations. The most well known of these is the organising of strategy around the use of 'tactical' nuclear weapons in Western Europe, a 'limited' and 'controlled' nuclear war to be fought with 'discriminating' and 'smart' devices, primarily in Germany. The notion that a war (which would actually destroy Western Europe) could be restricted to that threatre, and is in any way 'limited' or limitable is an absurdity which is certainly recognised by the Soviet Union, most European governments and past American Defense Secretaries.[32] The introduction of 'intermediate' range nuclear weapons – essentially rockets which could travel from Western Europe to the Soviet Union and in the opposite direction such as American Pershing–11s and Soviet SS–20s – made a nonsense of such an artificial notion of limitability.

Other writers have dealt plausibly with the doctrinal elaborations of strategy which give the dangerously ignorant impression that there is room for strategic manoeuvre in weapons policy. Draper's account of the seductive but mendacious character of 'escalation', 'options', 'flexible response' and 'counterforce' is a good explosion of this mumbo-jumbo which has come to have the status of sense at a high political level.[33] It is all rhetorical nonsense and empty fantasy which takes no real account of the weapons themselves and their practical uses, but which functions to mislead its audience into believing that it has some kind of autonomous control over the weaponry. It is a classic case of the divorce between politics and strategic reality.

Perhaps the most pernicious fantasy doctrine of all is that of the ability of one side to 'prevail' in a nuclear war, and thus to be able to sensibly consider fighting and winning.[34] This re-imports a pre-nuclear mentality into policy making which engages with the emotions and ideologies of a defunct militarism and which holds out, amid the deserved pessimism about war, the figment of national survival and recovery.

What is now accepted by the leaders of the USA is a concept of nuclear war as a credible option reinforced by a complete misperception of the weapons and an ignorance of the facts available about their likely effects. This is also the background context for negotiations between the superpowers to control the arms race. The irony is obvious. On the one hand we see a set of doctrines which stress war-fighting, and on the other a public facade which proclaims a desire to wind down that capacity. This explains the two features of arms talks which have made observers sceptical of their value in reducing danger: they depend upon an 'accountancy' process which tries to 'balance' what is already a superfluity of destruction, and they increasingly come to seem like the continuation of national struggle by other means – that is, the negotiations are themselves colonised by the geo-political struggle. Talks are about arms *control* rather than disarmament as such, and have had little effect on the arms race. Indeed we have reached the position where the process of arms negotiations is itself the secondary cause of conflict as it becomes absorbed within the propaganda campaigns to impute malign intentions to the other side in order to justify new weapons developments. This propensity of the armament process to dissolve all other aspects of foreign policy and national relations is the most significant development of all. It has culminated in the final position where the armaments themselves have become the *casus belli* – beyond all rational consideration of genuine national interest. The idea of a monster which comes to dominate its creator is over-used but it does seem appropriate here.

The conventional currency of discussion about 'security' and 'defence' which are usual in diplomacy and international relations have lost their old meanings in the nuclear age but they linger on to confuse us. The instabilities created by technological developments in the weaponry and by the inertial thrust of core sectors of social organisation depending upon the armament process are serious enough. Add to this the destabilising potential of the flux of international political alliances, the formation and disintegration of ties between societies and of sectional publics within societies, and the mixture becomes even more fissile. The growth of the peace movements on the one hand, and of a nationalistic 'new right' shift in governments on the other, both destabilise the situation. Thus events in Afghanistan, Poland, Nicaragua and the Gulf set up the grounds (but not the causes) for dispute, which is also affected by the dissension within NATO and within its separate partners over where interests lie and over the place of nuclear weapons in achieving those interests. The aftermath of even a relatively modest nuclear exchange will not recognise national boundaries.

Three dimensions of nuclear danger have been described. This is simply a means of illustrating the complexity of the issue and is not meant in any way to be exhaustive of the problems or to imply that each area should be seen as separate. It is meant as an antidote to the simple concentration on the aftermath of a nuclear war as somehow saying all that matters. The understanding of nuclear war as the horrors of its effects, which characterises popular debate, and the complexities of strategic doctrine, which dominate the political leadership, are both too important to remain publicly segregated in the way we have seen so far. The connection between both of these and the technical characteristics of the arms point towards a clearer appreciation of the meaning of stable deterrence.

DETERRENCE

Much of what has been said refers to the instability of

deterrence. It is the meaning and rational requirements of a system which deters the possessors of nuclear weapons from using them which is at issue here. How confident can we be in regaining and maintaining mutual deterrence? To answer such a question requires that we describe both the peculiarity of deterrence – its logical oddity – and its practical consequences.[35]

The significance of weapons as a deterrent is familiar: one party is dissuaded from being aggressive to another because of the fear of damage if the weapon is used. If both parties possess the weapon they may be mutually persuaded. All weapons have *some* deterrent effect, but given the uncertain nature of the precise harm which could follow the use of *conventional* arms, deterrence is usually extremely fallible. In the USA the right to bear conventional arms does not deter people from using them against each other because they think that they can get away with such aggression. Such a position could be described as one of 'inefficient' deterrence.

Nuclear weapons, because of their unique characteristics, have a totally distinct deterrent significance. To the extent to which they are treated as similar to conventional arms and with comparable deterrent effects they become uniquely dangerous. That is why it is most important to be clear what *nuclear* deterrence means. The effects of the use of nuclear weapons is different in kind to that following conventional ones in that no gain from an opponent's resources can be expected – the opponent's territory is destroyed by the use of the weapon – and the user of the weapon can expect, as we now know, to be destroyed by the effect of that weapon. The weapon cannot be used. It has no military potential whastoever except to deter an opponent from using it. This is the peculiarity of nuclear deterrence and its logical distinctiveness. After all, in no other field of human production do we construct things in order *not* to use them. None the less the paradox cannot be wished away that if we wish to deter others from war by the fear that we will use these nuclear weapons we must *appear* to be prepared to use them even though we both know that their use is impossible. The degree of irrationality in this position is clear. But to become rational and move away from such a MAD (mutually assured destruction) position requires that we disinvent the weapons, which is impossible, or, that we mutually disarm without disinventing which does seem exceptionally unlikely.

The paradox of nuclear deterrence splits appearance and reality. Appearance demands that we make our threat credible by developing weapons, preparing for war and elaborating aggressive doctrines as the display of our earnestness to use nuclear weapons if we have to. The reality is that we know more and more convincingly that we can never detonate nuclear weapons. This is nearly unbearable, which may go some way in explaining why appearance overcomes reality for some leaders as a way of restoring a sense of cognitive order.

Minimal nuclear deterrence exists when each side has the ability to retaliate to a nuclear attack with a nuclear 'second strike'. Such an ability has resided for some time in the 'triad' of launch positions for nuclear weapons where both super-powers can deliver a strike from long-range aircraft, land-based missiles or from submarines. This redundancy of threat guarantees a retaliatory capacity until it is possible to eliminate all three, a possibility which seems remote. Given this redundancy, and also given the very low threshold of detonation at which a nuclear winter would be threatened, all increased numbers of warheads, all sophistications of delivery systems and all attempts at defences are absurd and not justified by any appeal to deterrence. In fact all developments in weaponry since this position was reached have threatened deterrence, at the very least by refusing to recognise it, and this has led to the position where appeals have been made to re-stabilise deterrence as the only credible way to reduce the threat.[36]

Can deterrence be a stable condition? Purely apart from its moral consequences, is it practical to work towards a condition of minimal deterrence, and if so could it be maintained in the long run? These questions identify a sort of middle way between two other paths through the nuclear war preparation which confronts us now. One path is towards general, complete and mutual disarmament via a range of strategies from exemplary unilateral renunciation to mutually agreed cuts by negotiated agreement. The other is to break the mutuality of deterrence by seeking a weapons advantage through technological development, such as the Strategic Defense Initiative, and impose order by threat. Both of these paths seem fraught with difficulty and danger. The first seems to be a fantasy which is blind to the social and political realities of our societies. The second seems to be an invitation to engage in a first-strike nuclear attack in the belief that the damage caused can be lived with. Thus a return to deterrence through mutually assured destruction may seem the least worst prospect.

Two considerations are involved. The first is about how to get there from here. This is essentially a matter of ending those conditions which de-stabilise deterrence, notably those weapon-system developments and those strategic doctrines which propose the possibility of a military advantage. This is tantamount to a 'freeze' on all development and testing, to be followed by a negotiated 'build down' of armouries to the nuclear winter threshold. Such a position had been forcefully recommended recently, but so far with little political effect. The second consideration is of how to maintain such a position, in other words of how to exempt arms developments from the superpower antagonisms that will remain. The issue that stands behind the reformative proposals of a return to minimum deterrence is of the containability of those social pressures which have led to the arms race – technological, social and geo-political pressures which were described above. A return to deterrence may be the desired path *faute de mieux*, but its prospects are none the less extremely fraught.

One writer describes the central feature of our modern problems as 'impotence in power'.[37] We are faced by problems the solutions to which evade our comprehension, let alone our ability, but for which we propose fantasy approaches. Unable to accept that we have no solutions which themselves do not generate problems of comparable intensity, we pretend to a power which is, in fact, a fantasy. The nuclear dilemma is a rich nutrient for fantasy. The dreams of the disarmers and of the star warriors are not of course comparably dangerous. The latter group, because they are 'in power', are engaged in a fantasy about control itself which risks the ultimate catastrophe. But universal disarmers are also guilty of romantic fantasies which are in danger of becoming almost frivolous in the face of the several dimensions of the nuclear danger.[38]

It is particularly difficult to think clearly and feel constructively about nuclear war. The psychological and cultural effects of the presence of nuclear weapons are unique to them, although much of our imagery is limited to what has been recorded in past conflicts. Our sensibilities are blunted, our imaginations arrested in the face of this ultimate horror and its effects and this is combined with, and perhaps, partly, the cause of the cognitive limitations which affect, particularly, nuclear policy-makers. Some psychologists have been revealing about the psychic effects of prospective nuclear war.[39] There is a fairly extensive set of research findings which report on the specific fears and anxieties about nuclear war which are experienced by children and adolescents.[40] The sense of powerlessness and the feeling of being unprotected in a situation out of control exists alongside all the preparations for adulthood, and consequently the extra sense that this may all be a sham. The effects of nuclear weapons on the sensibilities of children is simply the most poignant example. The mechanisms used by adults to cope with, that is to continue to live with, 'the bomb' display a range of 'adaptations' from denial and displacement through to a kind of what Lifton refers to as 'psychic numbing'.[41] All are devices which may permit individual coping and all find culturally acceptable resources and justifications. But none are collectively or culturally directed to the source of those anxieties and some, such as the cynical accepting or even 'welcoming' of the likelihood of the end, are actively supportive of it.

The peculiarity of nuclear fear, and hence the difficulty of facing it, is of *futurelessness*. The experience of previous wars, and especially the images that have been recorded from Hiroshima and Nagasaki, provide the basic material of our fear – injury, pain, loss and particularly the fear of invisible contamination. But the idea, exemplified in the nuclear winter projection, of total 'endness' unredeemed by any future for mankind at all, or relieved by a religious vision of transition to 'another' world, has no place, yet, in our cosmology. Some repression of the truth about nuclear destruction, it has been remarked, may be necessary to allow us to prepare for it.[42] If this is so, and the ambivalence and ignorance which we have seen surrounding past horrors support such a view, then all we can hope for are improved methods of *individual* coping in the face of the personal reactions to the prospect of annihilation. There seems little in the way of a developing *social* response or cultural formation beyond a stark horror. Those collective responses which we do see, in the peace movements and in organisations devoted to active protest or education about the nuclear prospect, must depend upon a social consciousness, emotional and cognitive, which has transcended both collective pessimism and individual despair. Compared with the mass of reactions, and, importantly, the perverse responses of policy makers, these are models of sanity. In comparing popular complacency (and its private costs) with the deeply ignorant optimisms of political leaders we seem to be comparing pathologies. It is notable that military and political leaders once out of office become significantly more frightened and constructive.[43]

A traditional view of war still dominates our thinking about international conflict. We are still preoccupied with the idea that there is a rationality to fighting, even though nuclear weapons have changed irrevocably the world in which this was once true. A recourse to warfare by states which possess nuclear weapons risks the complete annihilations of any territorial or political gain which was the object of such a decision. The numerous wars which have taken place throughout the world since the practical adoption of nuclear weapons have been examples of a progressive increase in that risk to a point where there is now an increasing realisation that a 'threshold' is being approached beyond which war loses any rational meaning in the relations between nuclear states. The willingness of Western leaders to even consider the use of atomic weapons – which has happened at least three times since 1950[45] – is evidence of the slowness of decision-makers to accept this fact.

The traditional view, associated with Clausewitz, that war is the continuation of politics by other means and is thus a rational and calculative social activity is now irrelevant, but plainly lingers on in strategic doctrines and rationales which are thereby vacuous but dangerously misleading. However it would be naive to pretend that simply because the weapons have changed, militarism will shrivel and die. All the evidence supports a view of militarism as a core feature of most human societies.[45]

Locating the centrality of war-making in our sort of society and in the context of an omnicidal armoury is plausible grounds for pessimism. Very broadly we can attribute war either to the innate propensities of 'human nature' – whether we call it biology, psychology or whatever – or we can see it as constitutive of society itself. We can say that mankind is 'naturally' warlike for some sort of evolutionist reason or because of the unavoidability of the release of 'primitive' social emotions. Or we can see social conflict between groups as part of the very character of group differentiation, as profound and as universal as the division of labour, and which can only be finally resolved by force. Particular variants on these two themes may become popular at particular times. For instance the view that war is a *masculine* phenomenon, and is a response to the essentially male drive to dominate and confront, is a version of the human nature position but one which tries to qualify and refine the meaning of 'human'.[46] The view, held by some Marxists, that warfare is implicated now, principally, in the capitalist and imperialist state system is, similarly, a way of specifying and unavoidable connection between war and a particular social formation.[47] All of these approaches stress at least the ubiquity if not the inevitability of war. But those stressing its social nature point to the variations in its provocation, its conduct, its consequences and even to its social functions. They thus give slightly more hope for an understanding which might help minimise it. But there is little sense within these general perspectives on warfare that it will disappear. The concepts and the vocabulary which we use – especially that of 'defence' – are locked into meanings which derive from a time when warfare could be seen as rational. There are no meanings to such a debate which can refer to the contemporary situation beyond those which are concerned either with the contents of minimal nuclear deterrence or which are deliberately introduced to move back to a non-nuclear military posture.

CHAPTER 8

MORE DANGERS: FOOD AND NUCLEAR ENERGY

The last chapter outlined why we should think of the danger of nuclear war as the major threat to us all, and the principal grounds for a reasoned pessimism. The threat is man-made and social. It is a consequence of our organised social relations with each other which have embodied technology as the main means of that threat. It is the linking of the social nature of the danger with its technological expression which is the unique form of the difficulty. In the case of nuclear arms it is the combination of the political rivalry of states, the economic and social penetration of weapons as profitable and bureaucratised, and the momentum of technological developments which gives the issue its disastrous fixity. It is the same combination which characterises our treatment of 'the environment'.

The term 'the environment' has been appropriated for some time now as a device, or a handy slogan to dramatise a range of issues. These can fix on pollution, the exhaustion of reserves, the abuse of natural processes and the willingness to ignore social or physical limits to using the biosphere as a basis for production, a receiver of waste or as a public consumption good. The term is elastic in its political and, especially, in its campaigning use. But all versions of it do refer to one shared feature – that societies are *damaging* their natural resources in ways it may be impossible to remedy.

My reason for selecting this area as a second condition of pessimism is that, like the nuclear weapons issue, our treatment of the environment displays the *irreversibility* of the damage we can do combined with the *intransigence* of the damagers. There is a degree of uneasiness, generally, in the treatment of the environment as a purely physical or natural entity. We also view it as a valid social phenomenon which depends upon variable social perceptions and meanings, and which is hedged by economic and political significances.[1] Environmentalists themselves can be divided between those who adopt an essentially asocial and technologically determinist view and those who see the remedy as changing how we live, think and evaluate in our communities.[2] A purely technical view of the environment has been an important basis for environmental anxiety, but it has attached to it an unspoken optimism about the possibility of a scientific 'fix' which seems decreasingly plausible. Indeed a faith in new techniques, say of energy production or of food variety, as responses to dangers in the environment have, themselves, deposited new layers of peril on the original problem. A view of environmental danger, not as an issue of technology policy or as an act of God, but as a political and economic problem is increasingly necessary and obvious in the literature. It is also the most profound cause for concern.

The reason for this is simply our poor record in remedying what we know to be at fault. The *possibility* of technical change is, of course, always available. The *reality* has always been that our social organisation – our bureaucracies, managements, political organisations, cultures and ideologies – has proceeded even more forcefully in the direction that the same, increasingly sophisticated social organisation tells us is dangerous. One, sociologically informed view, then, of environmental danger is that it is the unlikeliness of genuine *social* change rather than the increasing evidence of unalterable physical damage to the environment which is the most worrying. Thus, for example, it is not just that we know more and more about how difficult it is to generate power using uranium or even plutonium-based reactors but that we seem unable to redirect energy production and use in order to avoid these difficulties. It is the sheer unresponsiveness of social organisation to new technical knowledge which is frightening, and the most persuasive examples of this can be seen in the now apparent failure of social and political movements, which are acutely aware of the new evidence, to have any effect on decision making. This issue will be described more fully in the next chapter. In this one I want to outline some fairly topical examples of how an understanding of the social causes of environmental problems is the basis of justifiable fears for the future.

It is increasingly difficult to speak about *the* environmental problem. It has always been a *port-manteau* term but it carries an expanding number of issues as the data on new precise dangers, and on the interconnection between already noted ones, becomes available. Texts on environmental problems deal with this range of areas by a strategy of simple accretion.[3] The centrality of particular issues such as population growth, the shrinking of mineral resources or the poisoning of the eco-system is a matter of chosen theory, or even political fashion, rather than some agreed or obvious set of core and peripheral factors. Therefore I will not pretend to describe what is of *prime* importance, since this is precisely what is at issue. But two sectors – food and energy – are of accepted general significance and are also the focus of dramatic public debates at the moment. They are both central to 'the environment' as the carrier of our societies, and they both demonstrate the determinant immobility of social relations in the face of both great suffering and potential disaster. But before looking at these two issues as examples it is important to put the modern concern with environmental issues into some historical and sociological context.

'THE ENVIRONMENT' AS IMPORTANT

Although there has been a specialised, often elite, concern with aspects of the natural environment for at least a century,[4] it was only in the late 1960s that we saw the dramatic expansion of popular 'environmentalism' in pressure groups and in the general awareness of the environment as under some threat.[5] The focus of concern has broadly followed the publication of the future studies described in chapter 6 but with an increasing variety of kinds of environmentalism from reformists to alternative life-style proponents. Public conern, as distinct from focused social movements, has ebbed and flowed as the media have battened on to particularly dramatic problems.[6] But it is probably fair to say that awareness that the environment is now threatened in a variety of ways is higher than ever before. Professional attention has paralleled the popular and there is an expanding academic literature from physical and social science which becomes, paradoxically, more esoteric *and* more generally informative at the same time.

Although the intensity of anxiety about the environment has been episodic and dependant upon events, the persistence of the idea of the 'environment-at-risk' as a container for a variety of fears about the natural world is notable. This is true, not least, because of the overstated warnings given in the 'limits to growth' reports of the 1970s. These led to debunkings and consequently a scepticism about the possibility of such catastrophes. The environment functions as a blank sheet upon which is inscribed the particular fear of man's interference with nature which best 'fits' with prevailing circumstances. But the important thing to note is that dangerous circumstances always do prevail. That is, although environmental anxiety is always shaped by local perceptions and particular values, there is always an available *real* danger on which it fixes: it does not invent the danger itself. This is an important point because I want to suggest that there is for the social scientist an issue of 'fact' here about objective evidence for new dangers, which belief systems necessarily interpret variously, but which are none the less the real conditions for people's lives. The perception of hunger and malnourishment may be socially variable. It may be seen as a result of fecklessness by the sufferers or as the result of greed by their exploiters, but those who are hungry will die. In other words it is not *just* a matter of perception. The social scientist is interested in both these implied levels: he must look at the social location of those in danger and their audience and see how this affects their perception of suffering, but he must also take the suffering as real and try to understand the social conditions which sustain it.[7]

Over the last two decades the environment has become a central issue because the damage being done is real. It is now of great importance because of the accumulation of knowledge we have about this damage and the new data which is becoming available, which suggests that even the dangers we thought we did understand have greater potential difficulties attached. At the very least the hopes of remedying some of the problems we knew we had have been severely qualified, and our confidence in our ability to adjust is dented.[8]

This issue of real and perceived danger is important in understanding environmental issues as increasingly significant because of the fall in credence of earlier alarmism. It is almost a copy-book case of the boy crying wolf so often that his warnings are now treated sceptically. Yet the real danger is not only still with us but is getting worse, not least because the fluctuations in its perception have enfeebled organised attempts to deal with it. Two general examples may help. First we are continually 'discovering' new hazards such as the dangers of exposure to high levels of carbon monoxide or to 'low' levels of radioactivity which, in a simple sense, add to the number of pollution dangers as well as interacting with dangers we already know about.[9] There is no reason to think that we have any reasonable estimate of the totality of man-made hazards to the environment or of the levels of their full effects. Second we are becoming more aware all the time of the profundity and extensiveness of those dangers that we have known about for ages. This is a result, in one sense, of simply extending the runs of data as time goes on because the longer we monitor a phenomenon the more we know about its character. But, in another sense, this extension of experience informs us of its *social* character and it is this last feature that I wish to concentrate on.

It is the social 'depth' and 'scale' of environmental abuse which can account for pessimism – the embeddedness, magnitude and interconnection of its social support. The crudest indicator of the penetration of damaging practices into the very ways of life of advanced industrial societies is the simple failure of control mechanisms over the last twenty or so years and the repetition and even increase in abuse. This is the new concern of environmentalist movements which are now somewhat weary of their lack of effect in anything other than cosmetic measures.[10] The reason for the immobility of the abusing system is that it *is* the system and that the exploitation of all forms of 'resource' is the basis, not just of industrial economies, whether capitalist or state-socialist, but of the technologies, consumption habits and dominant belief systems which underpin them as well.

In other words, although the symptoms are, for instance, the desertification of arable land, the exhaustion of forests, poisoned water and air, the mounting destruction of species, increasing hunger and the synergistic effects of all these combined, the pathology is the social organisation within which these can continue and even seem to remain 'functional'.[11] Although there is some hope in the relative success of some societies in tackling these issues,[12] this is less significant if seen against the global nature of the problems and the evident feebleness of international measures of reform.

It is our ability to control the production of environmental danger, seen historically, which is the most obvious marker of our potential to remedy matters. It is control, and the mechanisms which society has used to limit the manipulation of the environment, which are basic to any optimism we may have about the future. Yet it appears that control itself is subject to exploitation, both through its organisational domination by exploitative interests and, more subtly, through the confusion (perhaps mystification) of the very ideas of 'use' and 'abuse'.[13] The level of public debate about environmental problems is limited to quite local and selfish concerns within a very short time scale. This allows the idea of 'legitimate' use to be confined within a national and consumption based politics which is essential to the cycles of elections and the requirements of markets upon which, at least Western, democratic societies depend. There is a unity between the organisation of the state and the national economy which requires that issues which transcend their boundaries, whether of time of space, be relegated and downplayed, and certainly not be admitted as superordinate. Stretton remarked, a decade ago, that the use of resources is tied to social relations and that environmental costs are socially distributed according to those relations.[14] Those relations extend over the entire world and between generations. There has been no genuine commitment to examining inter-generational costs. The enormous debate about 'development' and the exploitation of less developed countries illustrates that even where issues of use and misuse are raised they are marginalised to academic debate and are absorbed, in practice, within the exploitative social relations which are the primary cause of the physical damage.[15] There is precious little hope that there are organisations and ideologies which can overcome this.

The power over the definition of 'damage' is interesting here. The role of scientists and science in the environment debate illustrates both the influence and the powerlessness of knowledge to change things. It was evidence provided by physical scientists working in particular sectors of technology or production that gave the early fears of environmental damage some credible substance.[16] The whole issue has always depended upon measurements of the effects on the physical world of social processes, and these are only within the control of scientists and technologists. At the same time, it is the impact of science and technology upon production processes, and its continual invention of new methods for the exploitation of nature, which is an important cause of the damage. This duality accounts, in some way for the ability of science alone to be considered as a fitting 'guardian' for the environment. In every-day terms the environment is considered to be some amalgam of the biological, chemical and physical world and *not* its surrounding social relations. The environment is seen in general public debate as the province of scientific specialists who are believed to possess the unequivocal 'facts' about damage and who are not partisan or 'contaminated' by values.

This is typical of the image of science and scientists in our culture and is connived at by scientists themselves.[17] It is also profoundly wrong. Just as scientists who choose to work on the developments of weapons have made a choice, based upon values, of the meaning of their science, so those scientists who work in areas which increase atmospheric pollution, or which actively attempt to decrease it, have also made a value choice. But they are certainly not generally perceived to have done so or see themselves in this way. Their image is still one of ethical neutrality and objectivity and, although this is increasingly difficult to maintain, it still dominates popular consciousness and guarantees scientists a moral and intellectual authority. Negative images of scientists drawn from fiction (Franken-stein) or recent history (animal experimenters or fabricators of damaging drugs) have little impact on the dominant positive impression with the result that scientists remain the sole trustees of the measurement of damage and hence its definition as serious. And, of course, to a degree, this is essential for who else can warn us, for instance, of the magnification of poisons in the food chain or the toxic effects of newly synthesised compounds? My point is an obvious and well known one that the *significance* of damage is a matter of social judgment and that control over the measurement of an effect is not a qualification for control over its public significance.

The science which warns us of the danger is that part of society which the state turns towards in order to control it. This has been the significance of the status of science in the whole debate. The existence of a growing body of 'enlightened technocrats' devoted to agencies and methods of *technical* coping seems to be the direction we will take. The popularity of 'environmental impact analysis' is one example but the growing number of especially international agencies attests to this faith in a science which, in public, at least, is untainted by the political structures which have caused the dangers and made them profitable, or otherwise socially required.[18]

All of these comments are at a high level of generality. They attempt to sketch in the social context within which environ-mental dangers are likely to increase and remain uncontrolled.

It is the very deep penetration into our social structure and relations of the abuse of nature which is increasingly evident. It seems unlikely that widely shared fears of damage will ever pierce the shell of a politically complacent willingness to risk long-term disaster for short-term convenience, a complacency which is cloaked with a scientific image to obscure its social features. Two examples should help to flesh out the direness of this situation.

FOOD

Our ability to feed the people of the world is decreasing. It is likely that more people will die of famine in the twentieth century than ever before[19] and most writing on the topic of food production and distribution is overwhelmingly pessimstic.[20] Hunger is a topical issue because of the attention given to famines by the mass media, and especially television, dating from the Nigerian/Biafran war of 1967–70. Widely transmitted pictures of starving children have ever since, and regularly, publicized the recurrent nature of hunger. The campaigns for aid to relieve the famines in Ethiopia and Sudan in 1985–86 are only the most recent, though certainly the most widespread, of the attempts to extend popular awareness of the existence of hunger. Unlike many other issues of inequality and unfairness, the maldistribution of the very means of life is exceptionally widely realised because of this. Yet what is publicly understood, beyond the bald fact of continuing starvation, is an explanation which itself contributes to the continuation of the problem, namely that starvation is the product of 'natural' forces and will thus always be present for emergency attention only.

Less developed countries are actually experiencing falling food sufficiency. For instance the food sufficiency ratio of sub-Saharan Africa was 98 per cent in 1961 and this had fallen to 78 per cent in 1978.[21] At the same time food imports there increased by over 8 per cent annually. Yet the world production of food is increasing : between 1970 and 1980, the

FAO tells us,[22] rice production went up by 30 per cent, wheat by 40 per cent and maize by 50 per cent. Most people in Western Europe are wearily familiar with the dairy and other surpluses accumulating over the last few years as a result of the EEC Common Agricultural Policy. In other words, continuing undernourishment co-exists with startling increases in overall supply: we see mounting productivity by North American wheat farmers at the same time as estimates of about one person in six in the world remaining undernourished. These figures are very general, it is true, and they allow a great deal of quibbling about what 'undernourishment' might mean,[23] but they are of sufficient magnitude to provoke a sense of righteous disgust, even allowing for likely qualification. They have produced some of the most articulate and forceful disgust refashioned into constructive programmes for over a decade now but with so little effect as to turn shock into outrage.[24] It is the persistence and even worsening of the problem in the face of widespread concern that makes the food issue a revealing example of the recalcitrance of environmental exploitation described earlier.

How can continuing famine be explained away? How is its recurrence treated as its inevitability? Only by the dominance of explanations which serve those *social* arrangements which use food as a weapon and as a source of profit or political control, rather than as a humane right. These explanations make reference to 'natural' forces which can only be respected and never modified. The strongest example of such an explanation is that which treats famine as the outcome of population growth, or rather 'overpopulation'. This is the contemporary version of Thomas Malthus' theory that population always increased faster than the food supply available to sustain it and that it was always stabilised by war, famine and disease. It is a doctrine which makes sense in terms of the debates at the end of the eighteenth century, but its persistence is harder to understand.[25] Apart from particular areas (such as Bangladesh), there is no 'overpopulation' in terms of the *capacity* of the areas in question to support their populations. Density of population does not correlate with the supply of food in general, and there are instructive cases of famine decreasing as population expands, as has been the case in modern China. In those areas of the world suffering the worst hunger, such as in parts of Africa, simply reducing the population will not increase food production. In global terms the 'carrying capacity' of the earth's surface, that is, how many people it *could* support if distribution were equitable, has been regularly uprated, and is certainly, at a *minimum*, five times larger than the present population.[26] So deeply is a vulgar Malthusianism embedded in our popular conceptions of population growth that the implications of this revision are hard to accept, and not least because if we abandon this doctrine of 'natural' limits about which we can do nothing we must face the issue as one which is, theoretically, within our control. Primary food production has grown more quickly than population, but not *where* the population was growing most rapidly. Food scarcity means a bad distribution, which is notionally changeable, rather than insufficient production which would appear to be much harder to remedy.

Other 'natural' explanations such as climate, variations in soil type and ecological disasters are all relevant only as marginal features of the problem. They are all pertinent at particular times and places but cannot explain the extent and character of world hunger and its persistence.

To understand the food problem as one of maldistribution rather than scarcity requires that we look to the social organisation of food consumption over the world, and that we see food for what it has become socially. If food means power, and not just sustenance, our sense of outrage – our *moral* view of the significance of food – must connect with an understanding of the true changelessness of starvation, its profoundly ramified and deeply entrenched basis. The residual optimism – often expressed as a sort of puzzlement without despair, a bafflement that believes 'things cannot continue like this for ever' – rests on the belief that hunger is eradicable given the right amount of determination combined with technological improvement.

Decades of attempts to reduce world hunger show little

success. The depressing history of food policies of various kinds supports a view that hunger in the world, as a practical issue, is resistant to our moral outrage. A policy based upon technological improvement and particularly 'Green Revolution', whether through improved varieties of seed or the techniques of cultivation, has been shown, in nearly all cases, to run counter to the much stronger economic and political structures in hungry societies.[27] The constraints on food production are only secondarily technical and owe much more to the web of exploitative relations in which the food producer is enmeshed. The need for fertiliser, pesticides or better processing facilities is certainly evident, but becomes irrelevant if the incentives for, and utility of, increased productivity is already crushed because the dominant interests in that society are to maintain things as they are.

Other directions for food policy are comparably difficult. Aid and development schemes and trading cartels of primary producers have done little but remedy the worst excesses of a system into which they fit, rather than effectively challenge. Genuine rural development, which is increasingly the agreed basis of any effective change for the better in the Third World, is certainly not the direction which most patterns of social change in those societies display.

Hunger is fixed because it is the necessary outcome of political relations between rich and poor societies. For it to be reduced, only those massive social changes need to happen which are the least likely to occur. The functional 'depth' of hunger – the way in which it 'fits' all levels of social relations and organisation except those which physically experience it – can be briefly stated. At the topmost level the superpowers, and especially the USA, use their command over food production as a tool of political control. Thus US grain price-support policy is used to fix production at levels which it finds appropriate, not only to allow it to sell grain to USSR, or otherwise on the world market, but also to satisfy internal political demands from mid-Western farmers, or to shore up the dollar or, indeed, whatever its *political* interests are perceived to be. Food, at this level, is a commodity with an exchange value. At the bottom level the peasant farmer in a poor country is bound to a system which requires food to be produced as a marketable good largely for export. The food goes to those markets which can afford it and not where need in nutritional terms is greatest. In between these two levels the peculiarities of fattening livestock on Third World grains for Western consumption (or of Soviet meat produced from US grain) with its huge inefficiency for protein production, and the increasing dominance of a capital-intensive agri-business, which destroys the soil and the variety of species, can be seen to be 'rational'. Hunger becomes fixed into international relations, cultural preferences within wealthy societies, bureaucracies, markets and ultimately into the declining capacity of those who pay the price to resist. The hungry cannot buy food because they are poor and this condition is necessary, legislated, intended and basic to the perceived interests of those with full stomachs.

Against this historically solidified fixity of hunger the prospects for reform are not great, especially given that all the secondary problems which aggravate food poverty – local population imbalances, climatic changes, emergencies created by wars – have an increasing multiplier effect upon the primary cause. The international organisations, which since the early 1970s have been concerned specifically with the world food crisis, have to contend with a global economic system from which they cannot escape and within which they can only hope to provide an emergency service which itself has to grapple with more and more intractible food disasters. As famine is the result of the lack of appropriate development in the poorest countries of the world, so these organisations must cope with first-aid field distribution in circumstances which make even an emergency service impossible.

The food issue illustrates that environmental abuse is a profoundly social matter and, because of that, very difficult to change. Agriculture is based upon depletable resources which are being 'consumed, extinguished and eroded at unsustainable rates.'[28] The continuation of the appalling mistreatment of undernourishment and hunger via a misuse of the land is evidently a social and political matter. The limits to the humane treatment of the starving, using the land, are social and this is the real basis for a pessimism about world hunger.

ENERGY

It has become a misleading commonplace that the world is short of energy. Before oil prices were raised by OPEC after 1973 energy costs were relatively unimportant in the cost structures of industrial economies.[29] The consciousness raised at this time was partly economic, and about the relativities of energy costs in international competition, and partly genuinely environmental, and about the potential exhaustion of fossil fuels and their more benign alternatives. This mixture has characterised debate about energy policy ever since, and has come to confuse and generally muddy the waters in the arguments over the place of nuclear power generation. For it is the issue of the future of electricity generation through the medium of nuclear reactors which is the most central issue here. In the aftermath of the Chernobyl reactor accident in the USSR in 1986, the worst nuclear accident the world has ever known, there is probably more public consciousness of the potential for catastrophe through the misuse of this technology than ever before. This coexists with an entrenched scientific and economic establishment, particularly in the UK and in France, which has a huge political and organisational invest-ment in nuclear energy. As political parties throughout Europe seize upon the place of nuclear power as a dominant election issue,[30] it has become the sharpest example of the division which characterises our view of the environment: it marks the fault line between those well-organised social interests prepared to risk enormous environmental damage for the sake of economic competitiveness, and those more fragmented sections of society willing to accept the costs of low economic growth for the sake of avoiding nuclear accidents, lower level radiation effects and the 'nuclear state'.

All energy production has environmental and health problems attached to it. We are learning more and more about the damage caused by the sulphur dioxide emissions from coal-fired power stations, about carbon monoxide and lead pollution from car engines, and plainly the building of wind-powered generators, tidal barrages and large-scale solar collectors all have significant damaging effects on the environment. We are mainly concentrating here on the production of electricity, as the most important vector of energy, and thus we are engaged in comparing the social costs and benefits of the use of fossil fuels, nuclear reactors of various forms and a variety of 'alternative' power sources, principally wind, tides, sun and geo-thermal. The major sources of electricity are and will continue to be coal and oil and indeed, together with gas, they form about 80 per cent of the world's total energy supply. Although there is some disagreement about what the 'exploitable' reserves of these energy sources are there is no 'crisis' in the sense that these finite resources are now being dangerously depleted. Such an idea of depletion is itself an economic and not a geological or environmental judgment. That is, when reference is made to some crisis of supply what is actually being said is that the costs of exploitation and delivery are deemed too high, not that the energy is in any strict sense unavailable to us. In other words the 'crisis' is one of choice and concerns who will pay. It is not about the end of our sources. Fossil fuel resources have always been understated. The discussions about the future of coal as a primary energy source, which have been particularly pertinent in the British case,[31] illustrate that our energy problems are officially restricted to those of pricing, and particularly the contribution of labour costs to that price. New mines opening up in Colombia, Indonesia and Botswana indicate an increasing supply potential but only acceptably so in market terms because of the low labour costs.

To take this issue of an 'energy crisis' slightly further, neither is there an acute problem of energy demand. Although there has been a consistent increase in energy use of about 2 per cent each year in the world as a whole since the mid-nineteenth century, this went up to 5 per cent per year between 1950 and 1973. But these rates of energy use were related to increases in economic growth in a period of relatively low real energy prices. The relation between energy consumption and economic growth has been shown not to be an invariant one, but to depend upon the relative real prices of energy and the incentive for technical efficiency in energy use.[32] The pattern of the use of energy to maintain or increase production and transport depends upon how a society pursues cheaper alternative sources of that energy and on the dominant pattern of production. Thus the context in which we should consider the nuclear power issue is not one of looming danger or of threat to the energy basis of our daily lives. It is one of the international economic competitiveness of the cost of energy in production. It is against this background that we should examine the potential of nuclear generation to itself create problems of a much greater magnitude.

Nuclear power stations only provide about 1½ per cent of end-use energy at the moment, and are not expected on any realistic estimate to generate anything more than a marginal proportion in the UK.[33] Also we have over thirty years' experience, in Britain, of commissioning and operating nuclear power stations, purely apart from that available from other states. So the experiential knowledge base is good, even if the proposed technology is still poorly understood, and the contribution it is proposed to make is minor in scale. Given these two background factors the technical and social risks of nuclear power are overwhelmingly dangerous. The term 'risk' has some technical connotations which I will describe in a moment. But first it is important to be clear about the general categories of risk which stem from the technical peculiarities of nuclear reactors, and which are not shared by other energy sources. These risks can be crudely divided into radiation, accidents and waste disposal.

The general dangers of exposure to nuclear radiation are well publicised. However the precise connections between health and levels of exposure to particular kinds of radiation are still matters of controversy.[34] The lethality of radiation at low levels of exposure is still being assessed and the precise connections between very low level exposures and particular cancer or tumour risks is not clear.[35] What does seem to be the case is that estimates of the 'safe' level of exposure are being reduced, that levels regarded as safe vary between states and that the risk from even marginal increases in radiation above the 'normal' background level may be greater than hitherto accepted.[36] The precise levels of these risks from radiation are not established by science and, indeed, it may be impossible to do so. But what is important here is that there is a risk at all, and the conditions under which it is manifested. There are essentially two conditions inherent in nuclear power generation which give rise to this risk – accidents of various kinds from catastrophic melt-downs of the nuclear cores of reactors to the unintended releases of irradiated materials; and the essential disposal of radioactive wastes collected as a result of nuclear power generation.

The record of accidents in nuclear power stations has come under increased scrutiny since the Chernobyl accident of April 1986. Accounts of the major incidents are available[37] although the delay of some thirty years on the release of full information on the Windscale fire of 1957 casts some doubt on our ability to scan the complete range of relevant data. However what is apparent throughout the range of accidents is the inability of even the most sophisticated technology to control *human* failure. Accidents have occurred in all major categories of reactor design and some of these have nearly been catastrophic. The Chernobyl incident has been the worst accident that has been admitted to have occurred so far and here also it now seems plain, from what literature is available, that it was the operator error in switching off emergency shut-down systems which caused the accident.[38] Nuclear power generation rests on the most complex technology that we have, and although there are engineering arguments about the variations within it – about whether gas, water or sodium cooled, pressure-tube, pressure vessel or unpressurized vessel, and now thermal or fast-breeder reactors are 'better' – none can be expected to be accident free.

The judgment of the risk of accidents is central to a

judgment of the acceptability of nuclear power. Chernobyl has concentrated our attention wonderfully on the 'large consequence, low probability' accident for which predictive models have been constructed, but within which the estimates of damage are hugely variable.[39] The acceptability of risk is a social and not a technical matter, but it must be based upon some values, usually mathematical, given to the various categories of risk. The risks of nuclear power can then be compared with the risks of alternatives and this is what is often done by proponents of nuclear power when they try to show that, for instance, coal fired power has just as serious consequences for overall health. Yet we should be aware that it is very difficult indeed to make such comparisons as some writers have noted.[40] Three difficulties are of immediate relevance here.

First is the very small amount of data available on which to measure the frequencies necessary for calculating statistical probabilities. Nuclear power stations have been around for too short a time for us to have any actuarial confidence in their record. Second is the persistence of the consequences of any major accident over time. The yield in fatal and non-fatal cancers from radiation exposure can only be seen over a period of a full lifetime – say seventy years – and even over generations in the genetically transmitted defects that may result. This strikes me as the most serious of the hard-to-estimate risks, and also that risk which makes nuclear power strictly non-comparable with other forms of energy generation, namely that the temporal (let alone spatial and physical) consequences are likely to be uniquely disastrous. Estimates of the long term effects of the Chernobyl accident given to the International Atomic Energy Authority have allowed a figure of 24,000 fatal cancers alone. The third difficulty is that of estimating the one common factor in all recorded accidents, that of human error.

These three difficulties mix up the *estimation* and *evaluation* risks. The first and third are about how we give a probability to an accident occurring. The second is about how we value that risk in terms of its consequences. It is this factor which makes it impossible for us to compare nuclear power with other forms. In other words we know that *if* a major accident occurs the consequences are exceptionally appalling. If we accept this, then even the very low estimates of the probability of an accident happening, which have achieved official recognition, pale into judgmental insignificance when set against their consequences. Although I have concentrated on catastrophic failures in reactors the range of possible accidents which result in the release of radioactive material into the environment is great. The unintended escape of radioactivity into the sea or into the air around power stations, as well as the contamination of workers within the plants, all add to the peculiar hazards to public health of this applied technology.

One particular technical risk which should be noted concerns the techniques of disposing of radioactive waste materials. It is a topical example of how a potentially dangerous aspect of nuclear power is officially marginalised, even though there is no technological solution to the problem available. Indefinite storage of high level waste is what disposal means at the present level of knowledge. Tank storage is used as an intermediate measure and there seems no solution in sight but to saddle future generations with the problem of 'stewarding' this exceptionally dangerous material, probably in vitrified form in some kind of underground vaults. Popular resistance to living above such dumps reflects the general dissatisfaction with the technological and social implications of this new burden. Sites on which low and intermediate level waste has been buried have also been shown to be less secure from the leeching of material into surrounding soil and water than had been assumed. The distinctiveness of the waste 'management' problem is that it illustrates a determination to press on with the technology *in advance* of reasonable confidence in its security. These are all risks implicit in the technology. What needs to be added to this to gain a fuller picture of the unique dangers of nuclear power are the *social* risks which arise as a consequence.

The gap between what Jungk calls 'the bureaucratic projection and the everyday reality' of nuclear power[41] is filled with the organisation of a repressive social control. The 'security' requirements of a nuclear state require that all aspects of the nuclear fuel cycle be policed. This is both to maintain the levels of actual obedience in work tasks in nuclear installations which the technology demands, and also to prevent nuclear materials being stolen for criminal or political purposes. The civil liberties implications and the subordination of most notions of formal or actual justice to the necessity of containing radioactive material are fairly obvious.[42] Thus the social risk is that the technological tail *must* wag the governmental dog and that conventional democratic rights and freedoms must wither in the face of the overwhelming need for 'security' before all else.

The connection between the civil nuclear fuel cycle and the military need for plutonium is a further aggravation of these social risks, as well as a contribution to the risk of nuclear warfare.

The social risks are all the organisational, cultural and ultimately behavioural changes that follow from a reliance upon nuclear energy, even at the margins of total energy production. Their outlines can only be seen dimly, now, in those changes already brought about by the nuclear establishment, and visible particularly in some of the campaigning techniques used to persuade government and public opinion of their necessity. But although unclear in detail and although we must project our fears and often be hypothetical, the *possibilities* are evident. The unique risks of nuclear energy are exceptionally severe. Do the likely benefits justify the taking of such risks?

The benefits assumed for nuclear power are economic. The environmental arguments used by nuclear proponents are very much an afterthought and a public relations device in a context where economic 'need' is plainly debatable. Sweet has argued that the economic benefits of nuclear power are illusory if a full account is taken of such factors as the enormous cost overruns on construction of nuclear power stations, and the generally low actual output of electricity compared with design potential.[43] The operational characteristics of actual nuclear stations as distinct from projections of possible performances, has always been disappointing. If we add to this the singular fact that the economies of nuclear power depend upon the prices of alternative fuels, economic superiority becomes much less certain. Further, if we add in the 'hidden' costs of cleaning up pollution and accidents, which must also apply to other fuels, and also the cost of insurance against accident (which is kept artificially low in the nuclear industry at the moment), the accounting procedures used to persuade us of the economic necessity of an increase in nuclear generation become less persuasive. If the actual costs are significantly more than official estimates suggest, the economic argument is not enough to sustain a case in the face of the enormous human risks involved. Even if the economic case were overwhelming it would not be enough. As it is we need to search elsewhere for the persistence of the pro-nuclear case.

It is the social organisation of nuclear interests which sustains this programme. The economic gains are not for society as a whole but for those corporations which manufacture and supply the huge range of goods and services needed to generate nuclear power. The situation is comparable to the 'military-industrial complex' which dominates weapons provision in that the unity of influence between commercial and political interests, appealing to 'science' as its ultimate rationale, seems unstoppable. The levels of decision-taking prior to the democratic process, or even open debate, are often remarked upon.[44] The test of their hidden salience is the immunity of their decisions both from public opposition and genuine market forces. The place of science and technology within the nuclear energy establishment is as complicated as it is in weapons research and development, though its self-image is more plausibly benign here. The elaborate corporate structures, which the massive expenditures and characteristically long development times require, now have, because of this size, reach and internal complexity a considerable degree of autonomy. The scientific research and development effort provides careers, prestige and an apparent independence for scientists provided they can explain away the risk factors as justifiable. The only plausible intellectual basis for this is the faith that science itself wil yield techniques to cope with the new risks it has produced. But faith is all this is and there is little rationality in continuing to produce new risks in advance of indications that the faith is justified.

It is tempting to treat technologies as intrinsically benign or threatening. This is an unsociological approach. The reasoned view of all knowledge is that it is in its use that it becomes social. Science and technology, and specifically nuclear technology, are no different. Yet it does have inherent characteristics with obvious social implications. To emphasise the benign potential without balancing this with the equally inherent risk is irrational, and in this particular case the singularity of the risk makes nuclear technology too dangerous now. The price which is being paid in health and environmental terms, and the price which could be paid are too high at present states of knowledge to justify extending the nuclear option when other definitely less risky alternatives are potentially available.

But the momentum of the nuclear programme is impressive, particularly so in the face of the Chernobyl accident which could be thought to be a signal warning. Yet the political and economic investment in nuclear energy, particularly in Britain, is so great that the nuclear public relations campaign is already trying to marginalise Chernobyl as a one-off incident which is untypical of the industry.[45] It is the *social* formation of nuclear energy technology which underwrites its central place in our energy policy.

This chapter began with a focus on the irreversibility of damage to the environment and the intransigence of those doing the damage. There are many other examples of this connection in the environment beyond the food and energy issues, but all seem to display the social promotion of technological danger or the social prevention of technological benefit (as in the case of food). In the past the four horsemen of the apocalypse – war, plague, famine and natural disasters – were regarded as uncontrollable. The modern period has been regarded as one of the steady extension of potential control over these dangers and this belief has been a central pillar supporting the whole edifice of 'progress'. Science, both as knowledge and as a set of institutions, both of which penetrate deeply into the substance of our society, has been central to this change. Yet what we now see is the addition of a fifth horseman – environmental catastrophe – which is man-made, and the probable aggravation of some of the others through the medium of that same social organisation which can promote their mitigation. For the extensiveness of social organisation, its efficiency, in short its potential for control, is constrained by the context of *the competition* in which it has grown. This competition proceeds at every level from the international to the local and is the superordinate social condition which we cannot avoid in our understanding of the shaping of our technological capacity. It is only such an assumption which can make sense of the acceptance of 'lifeboat ethics' and even 'triage' as the likely, perhaps even present, response to world hunger[46] and as the basis of our continuing with a uniquely high risk programme of nuclear power generation in the face of manifest lack of real need.

CHAPTER 9

NEW MOVEMENTS?

The burden of what has been said so far is that the grounds for pessimism are social. In the cases of the most serious issues facing us – the possibility of nuclear war, our inability to feed the hungry and to generate safe energy – it is the social relations underlying the use of technology or the social structuring of competition which seem the least reformable aspects. Technological developments are increasingly the means, and sometimes the occasion, through which these new threats are expressed, and it is the inherently destructive qualities of nuclear energy, to use the paradigmatic case, which is the very manifestation of danager. But, as is so often said, the technology itself is neutral. It is only a potential capacity and cannot be an active propensity until it is socially organised.

The main reason for deep concern about the social bases of these problems is their fixity and evident immunity from significant improvement. There is a common assumption that while technology is somehow 'hard' and a fixed feature of life, social arrangements are plastic and controllable. This is the common-sense version of technological determinism and it is a reversal of what we can see to have actually been the case. Basic social arrangements – social structure, behaviour, culture and even meanings – have changed very slowly indeed and then only in directions which have increased the competitive, predatory and exploitative potentials within social relationships.

Such a totalising judgment might seem absurd in this unqualified form. There are many accounts of social improvement deriving both from a general belief in social evolution, and from the standpoint of an acceptance of material consumption as the major index of well-being. It would be foolish to deny that for many people a number of aspects of life have been genuinely improved. But this must be seen against the new levels of 'disillusion, despair and destruction'[1] and against the zero-sum nature of these apparent improvements. Indicators of the 'quality of life' which go beyond consumption and material possessions are notoriously controversial, which is why consumption itself absorbs much of our everyday sense of well-being. However, such a limited perception degrades and mystifies the feelings of anguish and despair which we experience even when our material standard of living is high, and these feelings come to be seen as either personal pathology or as a 'cultural' malaise attributable to the sluggish adaptation of our sensibility to rapid material change. It is as difficult to use the rates of 'pathological' behaviour (crime, marital breakdown, mental illness, etc) to index a lowering quality of life as it is to use income levels to index its satisfactoriness. All that need be said here is that the idea that social change entails social improvement is unjustifiable, and that if we move from seeing society as simply the 'nation' towards a view which emphasises globalism, the interconnection between nations and supra-nationalism, then it becomes clearer that even material improvements are bought at a cost to others.

The deeper social determinants have not changed but are now amplified through new technical possibilities. The lack of evidence which could encourage an optimism about the potential for *social* reform is one powerful condition of gloom. It should not be confused, however, with an argument that social arrangements are *by their nature* fixed. This would be a fatalism of the worst kind and for which it is, anyway, hard to imagine adequate data. For all the concentration on patterns of social change by social scientists it is difficult to use the historical record to support any account of fundamental social improvement. History is the major potential source of information, which by and large provokes a sense of the timeless ubiquity of mutual depredation. While technical capacity and the ability to manipulate nature has plainly increased in scope and, up to a point, in depth, the social organisation which makes this ability real and actual is locked into patterns of competition which are becoming increasingly dangerous, as they are expressed in new technical forms. As technical reach outpaces social grasp[2] this inability to *really* change is potentially fatal.

The historical record is the most important place to look for signs of hope but we must make decisions about the time scale to be adopted. The despondency about 'historical' improvement increases with the period examined because we want history to 'teach' us from the fullest set of data available. This in turn means the piling up of a record of, at best, repetition and, at worst, randomness.

The only remaining source of an optimism about the social basis of our difficulties is that evidence which contradicts history: the evidence that an *unprecedented* change is now occurring. This means that we should look to those changes in social life inspired by the very peculiarity of our dilemma, to the *new* politics and social movements which have been provoked by these newly dangerous circumstances. Part of the argument proposed already is that we are in a situation without precedent, and that although history displays little evidence of strictly social change it does show us that we have reached a position of technical peril which is not a repetition of previous circumstances. In other words our social behaviour has never changed but the cumulative result of this changelessness has been a new ptich of danger. This sounds impossibly paradoxical but it does have an acute meaning. The novelty of the present is the scale of damage that technology has made possible combined with an inability to deal with that technology. The extent of the threat is the ground for a new sense of danger which, in turn, has consequences for political life. There may be a potential for genuine social change which is itself a consequence of a new level of popular anxiety, and this may be manifested in new forms of social organisation and new ways of life. These are a possible core of real social change.

NEW SOCIAL MOVEMENTS

The idea that the last decade or so has seen the rise of radically new social movements has been popular. Characteristic of this view is the hope that such movements in fact presage a new politics which can challenge the monolithic fixity of conventional systems, can innovate and present an alternative.[3] The major examples are the ecology, peace and feminist movements, but we could also include regional, ethnic and sexual minorities, urban movements, anti-racist and counter-cultural movements. All these are potentially important as specific challenges to dominant local systems, but are also seen as similar and mutually sympathetic versions of a general change in collective resistance and perhaps utopian, even prophetic, social improvement. In the search for antidotes to the tragic consciousness, which must follow from our present predicament, social movements are centrally important as centres of innovation and resistance. An assessment of the 'newness' of modern movements and an understanding of their origins, development and successes so far should help to locate a significant support for optimism.

The novelty of contemporary social movements depends upon an initial contrast between a 'new' and an 'old' politics. The latter is dominated by associations characterised internally by formal, bureaucratic organisation, general doctrine, shared beliefs and strategic policy formulation.[4] The field of conflicts in which these organisations work is primarily economic. The old politics is made up of stable organisations, themselves saturated with professionalisation and careerism, locked into an almost ritual conflict over economic growth. Social class struggle is the foundation of all such politics and within this model other antagonisms which cannot be read off from the economic are seen as trivial and peripheral.[5] There is a long tradition of cynicism about the ability of such organisations to do anything other than repeat the very political forms which guarantee that nothing really changes.[6] It is against this model that the new politics and new social movements are seen as important. The possibility of breaking this mould has only been apparent recently in the rising popularity of protest movements of various kinds, and the empirical research available is not very large.[7] But upon this slim data base rests considerable speculation, from a variety of directions, that what is happening is new.[8]

There have been several traditional theories accounting for collective action and social movements, the most powerful of which have been the collective behaviour and resource mobilisation accounts.[9] These have tried to explain social movements as predominantly responses to structural crisis and breakdown, as reaction-formations, and as collectivities united by shared beliefs and motivations which forge groups into united interest movements. These theories have had some difficulty, however, in explaining the peculiarities of the new social movements, and particularly their focus on issues like disarmament and the environment, and their exceptionally fluid forms of internal organisation. The idea that both the new forms of contemporary movements and their motivating concerns are linked gives rise to explanations which stress this unity – new models for new phenomena.

The new movements have a characteristic organisational form stressing multiple membership, part-time and short-term militancy and a high degree of emotional solidarity. There are a variety of types but they generally display 'a network of small groups submerged in everday life which require a personal involvement in practicing and experiencing cultural innovation'.[10] They are so-called SPIN groups (segmented, polycephalic, interacting networks), grass roots organisations populated not only by the young but by the 'middle layers' of state employees in the health, education and welfare services, at least in Western Europe.[11]

Examples come from a number of directions. Touraine's study of an anti-nuclear protest movement in France claims to show the group as an agent of significant cultural change, producing a counter-model of the 'post-industrial' society.[12]

Castells' accounts of 'urban movements' (for instance Dutch and German squatting associations, Italian and Spanish citizens' movements) were originally seen as major contemporary social movements organised around consumption issues and containing a transformative potential.[13] Rowbotham *et al.* make bold claims that grass roots struggles by a whole range of 'fragments' are shaping a new political practice.[14]

The very visible nature of these new alignments and tendencies has forced a rethink of the 'old' politics which could no longer explain the issues around which the movements crystallised, nor could it connect them with the social class, and especially economic issues which have been privileged by the left as the only possible bases for significant social change. The decoupling of political interest from class issues means that new criteria of political significance must be used, in other words a new politics to fit the new movements.

The oppositions between the old and the new are clear: formal organisation is replaced by non-hierarchical and spontaneous cohesion; social class is replaced by a whole range of multi-class or even non-class issues; bureaucratic and conformist behaviour is replaced by 'exemplary' patterns of living and alternative life-styles. This last issue is particularly interesting as it dramatises the profound difference between the old and new movements at the level of immediate sensibility and feeling.

The idea of politics as 'lived' is not new, and some social movements have always demanded that their adherents conform to particular codes of behaviour. But the idea of politics as *primarily* expressed through a way of life is a popular phenomenon mainly of the last twenty years. The very idea that politics is a matter of everyday life rather than some separate place and period, beyond the immediacies of domestic and personal existence, is evidence of how far the old politics had become inadequate for many, especially young, people. Given that the old politics had obviously not changed ways of life but had essentially reordered hierarchies within the old, it is not surprising that how life was to be lived should become both the issue and the means of demonstrating it. This connection of 'levels' is impressive. After a very long time in which politics was seen by nearly all as about material goods, and in which the life of the feelings was assumed to follow on from consumption, it was clear that rejection of 'economism', economic growth and even redistribution of income was demonstrable in individual lifestyles as well as a policy statements. The politics of the immediate and the personal, felt, lived and displayed, was a uniting of means and ends in a new way. The experience of a relatively affluent generation who could *choose* to live in communes, become 'hippies', not work for wages and engage in full time 'political' activity provided an early social experience which was traded on by later more serious social movements.

What have been called 'alternative ways of life'[15] can be seen as serious demonstrations of alternative human and environmental relations to be set alongside prescriptions of a more just international order. The connection is made between politics at a number of levels and between their associated strategies – from the personal level and the strategy of individual social responsibility, to the movement level and the strategies of reform or contestation. The immediacy of the engagement of the feelings, when lifestyle is treated self-consciously as a political statement, can be contrasted with the routine quality of conventional political activity in trade unions and mass political parties. Indeed it is only when these old forms become 'contaminated' by the new, as is increasingly happening on the left, that new energies are engaged there and new kinds of members activated.

Two questions remain to be answered about these new movements. Are they progressive? Are they effective?

PROGRESS AND VALUE CHANGE

The importance of the new politics and new social movements partly rests on the extent to which they embody radically new and progressive values. They are, at least potentially, important if their change in organisation and their concentration on new fundamental issues reflect value choices which are in some way superior or more appropriate for survival than those they challenge. Such an idea brings us back to the notion of progress which we saw, in chapter 4, was in some doubt if treated in a materialistic way. To ask how far new movements are a focus for a new conception of progress, or even just remedial examples of progressive social change, requires that we pay some attention to the very idea of a scale of values in which some can be seen as better than others. This is not a very respectable task for sociology where relativism about values is almost an article of faith. Indeed just to broach this issue is close to condoning some form of evolutionism with all the politically unpleasant judgments that could then follow.[16] However, as I have already abandoned relativism in describing contemporary problems as uniquely dangerous and not just part of some deeply repeating repertoire, an examination of values as fitting or denying these developments seems reasonable. Some values may be better than others in the sense that they may contradict social developments which we agree are potentially terminally dangerous.

Several models are available, particularly in the psychological literature, which specifiy hierarchies, scales and standards of both behaviours and values. These are potentially evaluative, and usually rest upon some notion of 'maturity' and 'growth' which, although it may have meaning when applied to the development through ageing of the individual human being, are not easily transferred to other entities like social groups. Probably the best known example of such a developmental hierarchy is Maslow's scale of needs.[17] This argues that individual needs are fulfilled in order of their contribution to survival – physiological needs first, followed by higher order needs for belonging, love, respect and so on, as the basic needs are fulfilled. By extension we might argue that the pursuit of lower level values is pathological in a situation where needs at this level have already been met, and that the expression of higher level values is thus 'superior'. Another example is Kohlberg's stages of moral judgment.[18] This creates a sequence of moral positions from the 'preconventional' – egocentrism – through the 'conventional' – individualism – to the 'postconventional' – a morality of human rights, social welfare and general ethical principles. This is a hierarchy of social values in which, once again, it is possible to see the persistence of individualism, and of competitive local interest as 'backward' or even 'primitive' in advanced industrial societies.

These are both possible models for the judgment of progressive social values. They provide, if accepted, a template against which the values of particular groups can be set and appraised. Just as we are familiar with the idea that an individual matures as he grows older, and that he can 'grow' and learn even as an adult (and there is, now, more popular acceptance of this through the techniques of humanistic psychology and forms of therapy), is it similarly appropriate to scale the values of social groups, such that we can speak of some as more advanced or progressive than others?

Some attempts have been made to use these models in describing the characteristics of groups in society now. Inglehart, using Maslow's ideas, showed that there was a generational change in Western Europe in which younger groups supported post-material values concerned with the quality of life, compared with the older generation's emphasis on material well-being and physical security.[19] The changed experience of adolescence though extended education and socialisation generally are located as the sources of this fundamental change. Kohr and Rader in West Germany have tested Kohlberg's moral judgment scale on large samples of German youth and have shown an increasing post-materialist, ecology-oriented conception of politics and a postconventional type of moral thinking.[20] They have, further, indicated that the peace and 'Green' movements play an influential part in youth culture with about one third of sixteen to twenty five-year-olds sympathising with both movements.

There is certainly a challenge to the 'master' values of economic growth, commercial culture and the Protestant work ethic from the new social and political movements and from their youthful membership. The sharpest point of this is the criticism of competition which, as was suggested in chapter 8, is the basis of our dangerous social relations. Additionally it counterposes co-operation and the priority of moral reasoning over calculative self-interest. But what is most important is that this opposition is not just one of intellectual paradigms. In addition it has strong emotional and motivational connotations; it is related to feeling and action both in the immediacy of the issues in which these values are manifested – disarmament, preventing environmental damage – and in the very forms of protest, struggle or innovation – demonstration, direct or emotional symbolic action, living 'alternatively'.

There seems to be grounds for calling the values of some of the new movements 'progressive', at least in the limited sense of a comparison with the values which inform the dominant paradigm.[21] The latter are by definition constitutive, or at least supportive, of the most severe threats to global survival we have ever experienced. The former are either reactive 'symptoms' of our distress or they are attempted solutions to the frozen social relations which underwrite the technological threats.

A SOURCE OF CHANGE?

Enough has probably been said to suggest the broad parameters of novelty of these social movements. But newness and progressiveness alone are insufficient evidence of potency. We see new conflict over new issues by new forms of organisation using new methods. But there is less clear evidence that they have been effective, so far, in moving us away from the danger. The measure of the new movements as a source of hope is not just their popularity, or even their persistence, but their success in shifting the old politics in a more benign direction. We look for evidence of real effects on the direction of the arms race and our exploitation of the environment but there is little sign of encouraging success. Two examples of potentially profound new social movements illustrate the resistance of dominant patterns of social organisation.

The peace movement in Britain, and particularly its core organisation, CND (Campaign for Nuclear Disarmament) has experienced a recent massive increase in popular support and mass participation indexed by formal membership and by the size of demonstrations. There is remarkably little research and published data about this movement and so any conclusions are necessarily more speculative than usual.[22] The current British peace movement is part of a much longer tradition of anti-war movements[23] but in its 1980s form it has been characterised by a revived resistance to the basing of 'Cruise' missiles in Britain and to Britain becoming a more heavily armed and more strategically vulnerable forward base for the USA. Its support has grown in proportion to the apparent increase in risk which has followed America's more obvious aggressive posture over the last few years. It is, thus, a highly focused movement with clear aims of resisting the siting of particular weapons but within the overall goal of complete disarmament. CND has a national and delegate organisation but is dependant upon its local and regional branches for action. These branches are themselves highly fissile coalitions of diverse groups – socialist, pacifist, religious, feminist, etc – united in a network with a minimum of 'official' positions or procedure. Additionally other peace movement groups, for instance the 'Greenham women' are sympathetically allied. It is quite clearly a 'new' movement in its modern form and is, perhaps, the most obvious source of popular pressure for a change in Britain's defence policy. And it has clearly failed in its immediate aims. Defence policy and practice has not been moved by CND. Public opinion has been highly changeable, in ways not clearly attributable to the peace movement. Cruise missiles have been installed and the British government has become even more closely associated with America's bellicose posturing in international relations, arms negotiations and in weapons development.

The 'Greens' in the Federal Republic of Germany are an even more popular and publicised new social movement and can be seen as the most likely candidate for practical change in the old politics. Founded in 1979 *die Grünen* crystallised out of mounting concern for the environment during the 1970s from a variety of directions – disillusion with social democratic programmes, the *Burgerinitiativen* (citizen pressure and action groups), resistance to nuclear power programmes and the faltering of the 'new left' organisations of the late 1960. The convergence of these tendencies and their consolidation into a form of coalition organisation to function, both as an extra-parliamentary but also an electoral opposition, culminated in the 1980s in unprecedented success in a number of elections and in the mobilisation of large numbers for demonstrations.[24] In 1983 the Greens gained over 5 per cent of votes in national elections entitling them to twenty-seven MPs in the West German Parliament. They became the first post-war 'party' to challenge the established three party monopoly. As late as 1984 they gained over 8 per cent of the relevant votes in the Elections for the European Parliament. This penetration of official politics was accompanied by a simultaneous distrust of that same system and an intention to 'use' it rather than become part of it. Green politics is oriented to grass-roots democracy and social justice as the means towards a radical change of society in an ecologically protective and socially egalitarian direction. It thus appears to be a quite unique mixture of utopian aims and pragmatic methods, and as such offers a model of such movements as being seriously reformative. The Greens are an organisation of the young[25] and attract their voters from the younger and more middle-class sections of German society, and largely those in health, education, welfare and personal service occupations. There is an over-whelming concern with democratic structures throughout the movement and the party, and an intention among all factions to demonstrate in organisational practice what is being proposed as a political goal.

The Greens also are failing. The deployment of Cruise and Pershing–11 missles, which was a dramatic focus for resistance by the Greens, has been carried out. The political and social policies of the Kohl administration have not noticeably shifted in any area in a Green direction, on energy, unemployment, industrial change or defence. Some of the electoral and ideological support for the Greens as a realistic opposition is now being switched to the SPD, as an 'official' party, and internal difficulties of structure and tactical policy have weakened the practice of opposition to the dominant political system. It seems likely that the Greens are in decline.[26]

On the very crude measure of effect on policy, neither of these movements provides a sign of hope. We can attribute their failure to local and limited difficulties, or to features intrinsic to this form of organisation. There are grounds for understanding the latter as contributing quite heavily to the current failures in both examples, and the lack of success in campaign goals is likely to exaggerate these enduring problems.

The Greens are faced with the difficulty of maintaining unity in a potentially fragmented coalition over time, while striving for a decentralised and grassroots form of democracy. These may be contradictory goals. The Greens are an amalgam of four factions. These are, first, the 'fundamentalists' exemplified by Rudolf Bahro[27] who are not interested in parliamentary politics but wish to maintain a demonstrative role of announcing an emancipatory consciousness; second, the 'political realists' who wish to promote more party politics and the accommodations with, for instance, the SPD that will permit greater leverage within the 'old' political system; third, the 'eco-socialists' who wish to increase links with class-conscious mass movements and with whatever seems progressive from a socialist perspective at the time but avoiding any clear links with the SPD; and finally the 'libertarians' who argue for political compromise with groups other than the SPD, who are on the conservative wing of the Greens and who are primarily afraid of the socialist road to ecological improvement. The tensions between these four factions are severe enough to have prevented any coherent and practical direction for the Greens since 1984. These difficulties at a group level have been magnified by the day-to-day absorption with internal structure and how the Green MPs should be organised, for instance the variably accepted process of 'rotation' of MPs who after a fixed period must give up their positions. These particular tensions represent the more general contradictions which are raised when the new movements wish to have an effect on the old politics. They are not peculiar to the Greens. They concern choices about goals and the means to achieve them which are enduring features of organised political activity which have been at least 'stabilised' in traditional political organisations, if not resolved.

The British peace movement and CND evince the same difficulties. Parkin's view of CND in 1968 that it was an alignment of diverse and disparate causes, as partly 'expressive' and 'symbolic' of other issues and interests, although it may not adequately characterise the movement now, does help us understand its essential difficulty in achieving campaign goals.[28] The difficulties of holding together diverse interests such as socialist, feminist and Christian groups at the local level only become apparent over time. Campaigning for particular objectives with a high degree of emotional commitment can submerge such tensions. But the failure to achieve those objectives reduces the superordinate motivation and the differences remain. If the issue alone must be strong enough to unite different groups then changes in this issue pose problems. In addition organisational methods which refuse to stress bureaucracy, officialdom or routine 'efficiency' provide little continuity when the issue fades or becomes confused. The irony here is that the opposition to hierarchy and political 'opportunism', which is a uniting feature of such movements, becomes a cause of failure to engage effectively with the official organisations which are founded on these features.

The only way out of these problems is for new social movements not to resist the old politics on its own ground if it can never win there in parliaments or the organisations of the state. This leaves domonstrative politics and extra-constitutional opposition as the only avenue and this requires mass mobilisation beyond the movement's conventional adherents, or small scale but tactical disruption. Neither seems likely or constructive.

Conventional politics has had little difficulty in resisting the force of new social movements. The lack of vulnerability of 'teflon politics' to environmental and peace demands has been startling and depressing.[29] Business continues as usual because in the end social movements are distant from or subordinated to the political system, as well as suffering internal breakdown.[30] The most that can be hoped for is a resistance which slows down some of the damage but does not reconstruct or innovate. The depth and spread of the social basis of our problems increases by the opposition it can overcome. Where else do we look for signs of real change?

CONCLUSION

Pessimism is the negative evaluation of the likely future. Although there are many areas of anxiety that I have not attempted to describe, the threats of nuclear war, increasing hunger and nuclear pollution are sufficient to deny the new pessimism as groundless. And there are enough indicators of professional and popular concern, enough evidence of the collapse of assumptions of progress and confidence and enough faltering of benevolent prospects to justify investigation into the new anxiety – though using methods sensitive to the emotional salience of the issue. Such pessimism is not superficial and is probably not local – only time will tell if it is transitory!

We can map this pessimism but we should surely go beyond this to assess its justification. The social location of optimists and pessimists will not be important if a nuclear war begins; sociological relativism will disappear along with everything else. But a wider understanding of pessimism can only help to avoid its worst predictions which is why, I suppose, in the end, this book is residually optimistic.

The deep structure of our difficulties is social. Although the manifestation of danger is technological it is the awful intransigence of our social processes, now expressed through these terrible technical potentials, which underwrites pessimism. Our knowledge of the feebleness of true social change and of the immobility of our social relations is impressive. The modern period is characterised by increasingly penetrating and extensive social disciplines which interrogate history for signs of hope but which reveal only expanding levels of familiar dangers, played out on broader stages. The longer we go on, the more we know about how little social processes have altered.

There is a potentially tragic irony here: the current coexistence of maximum danger and the greatest understanding of it in conditions where that very danger renders the understanding impotent. Social science provides the ironic commentary on the paralysis of knowledge in practice. The powerlessness of knowledge arouses yet more anxiety for those whose faith in the future has been founded on instrumental rationality, and this anxiety is expressed, as all anxieties must be, as *feelings* about the future. How are we to view the future if the only thing we know with certainty is that we seem unable to avoid the pits that we dig for ourselves?

The feelings which we are likely to have about the future, in these circumstances, are understandably cynical or despairing. The pathology of cynicism was described in chapter 4 as a contribution to the destruction which it prematurely assumed. Despair is no less dangerous in its abdication of all potential possibility. When Brecht described those who laugh as not yet having heard the bad news he illustrated the smothering and strangulating quality of such despair. This can only end in the suicidal, and perhaps even homicidal, embracing of a personal end in advance of the social one.

To truly abandon hope is plainly very difficult, for reasons of temperament which are social in nature. The obstinate hopefulness which most of us share and which we locate in our domestic, familial and local lives is the reservoir of constructive feelings which must, in some sense, engage with the future. We pay attention to the future there. We plan, organise, decide priorities and display altruism, co-operation and concern which far outweighs the conflicts and exploitations which are also evident; we love and care for our children much more than we abuse them. Our benign impulses can extend even further; we have given to the hungry on the other side of the world in an open and unforced access of communality. Our culture has within it rationales for constructive responses to the future. All possibilities are not closed off.

NOTES

CHAPTER 1 A NEW SENSE OF DANGER

1 Generally on this see Glasgow University Media Group, *More Bad News*, London, Routledge & Kegan Paul, 1980.
2 F. Kermode, *The Sense of an Ending: Studies in the Theory of Fiction*, Oxford, Oxford University Press, 1967, p.24.
3 This is put forcefully in P. Tallis, 'Is realism still relevant to modern reality?' *Listener*, 20 February 1986.
4 R. Nisbet, *History of the Idea of Progress*, New York, Basic Books, 1980, especially p.7.
5 This of course refers to K. Popper, *The Poverty of Historicism*, London, Routledge & Kegan Paul, 1985. For a fuller account see chapter 5.
6 Kermode, op. cit., pp.94–5.
7 The most well known expression of this view is Gramsci's contrast between the 'pessimism of the intelligence and the optimism of the will'. Q. Hoare and G. Nowell-Smith (eds), *Selections from the Prison Notebooks*, London, Lawrence and Wishart, 1971, p.175.
8 For instance the second law of thermodynamics which describes 'entropic degradation' – the continuous and irreversible shift of the universe from order to disorder.
9 G. Orwell, *The Collected Essays, Journalism and Letters of George Orwell*, Harmondsworth, Penguin, 1970, vol. 3, p.280. This is a review written in 1944 of a book by Arthur Koestler and is a fertile source of Orwell's views on short-term pessimism and long-term optimism and on the significance of time.
10 E.P. Thompson, 'Notes on Exterminism, the Last Stage of Civilisation', *New Left Review*, no.121, 1980, pp. 3–27.
11 As is the case in R. Aronson, *The Dialectics of Disaster: A Preface to Hope*, London, Verso, 1983. This is otherwise an interesting and

relevant account of the grounds for pessimism – in spite of the title.
12 See for instance D. Rowe, *Living with the Bomb*, London, Routledge & Kegan Paul, 1985; R.J. Lifton, 'Imagining the Real: Beyond the Nuclear End', in L. Grinspoon (ed.), *The Long Darkness: Psychological and Moral Perspectives on Nuclear Winter*, Yale Conn., Yale University Press, 1986; J. *Macey, Despair and Empowerment in the Nuclear Age*, Philadelphia, New Society Publishers, 1981.
13 Aronson, op. cit., p.257.

CHAPTER 2 THE SOCIAL STATE OF MIND

1 For a general statement on this see A. Giddens, *The Constitution of Society*, Cambridge, Polity Press, 1985, pp.28–34.
2 A formalisation of this is seen in Schutz' 'postulate of adequacy'. A. Schutz, *Collected Papers*, The Hague, Mouton, 1967, p.44. For an assessment see A. Giddens, *Central Problems in Social Theory*, London, Macmillan, 1979, pp.246–8.
3 M. Oakeshott, *On Human Conduct*, Oxford, Clarendon Press, 1975, pp.31–46.
4 R. Williams, *The Long Revolution*, Harmondsworth, Penguin, 1965; *The Country and the City*, London, Chatto & Windus, 1973.
5 W. Lepenies, 'Cold reason and the culture of the feelings', *Social Science Information*, vol.24, no.1, 1983, pp.3–21.
6 T. Parsons, *The Social System*, London, Routledge & Kegan Paul, 1956, pp.11–13.
7 Giddens, 1984, op. cit., pp.41–51. Also see N. Thrift, 'Bear and Mouse or Bear and Tree: Anthony Giddens' Reconstitution of Social Theory', *Sociology*, vol.19, no.4, 1985, pp.609–23.
8 See S. Giner, *Mass Society*, London, Martin Robertson, 1976.
9 K. Mannheim, *Ideology and Utopia*, London, Routledge & Kegan Paul, 1960 (1936).
10 N. Stehr and V. Meija (eds), *Society and Knowledge: Contemporary Perspectives in the Sociology of Knowledge*, New Brunswick, Transaction Books, 1984.
11 R. Williams, *Towards 2000*, London, Chatto and Windus, 1983, p.266.
12 J. Habermas, *The Theory of Communicative Action*, London, Heinemann, 1984, vol. 1, section 3. Also see the variations on this theme in the work of Fromm and Marcuse.
13 For instance H.J. Gans, *Popular Culture and High Culture*, New York, Basic Books, 1974.
14 R. Nisbet, *History of the Idea of Progress*, New York, Basic Books, 1980.
15 T. Noble, 'Recent sociology, capitalism and the coming crisis', *British Journal of Sociology*, vol.XXXIII, no.2, 1982, pp.238–53.

16 Such as N. Cohn, *The Pursuit of the Millennium*, London, Paladin, 1970.
17 See P. Brantlinger, *Bread and Circuses: Theories of Mass Culture and Social Decay*, Ithaca N.J., Cornell University Press, 1983, ch.5.
18 Notably and not completely convincingly F. Parkin, *Middle Class Radicalism*, Manchester, Manchester University Press, 1968.
19 For a commentary on this see T. Scheff, 'Intersubjectivity and Emotion', *American Behavioural Scientist*, vol.16,no.4, 1973, pp.501–22.
20 D. Rowe, *Living with the Bomb*, London, Routledge & Kegan Paul, 1985, ch.2.
21 Lifton has written extensively on this subject. From a great deal of relevant material see R.J. Lifton and R. Falk, *Indefensible Weapons*, New York, Basic Books, 1982.
22 B. Tizard, 'Can children face the future?', *New Society*, 12 September 1986, pp.9–12; S.T. Fiske *et al.*, 'Citizens' images of nuclear war', *Journal of Social Issues*, vol.39, no.1, 1983, pp.41–65; M. Schwebel, 'Effects of the nuclear war threat on children and teenagers', *American Journal of Orthopsychiatry*, vol.52, 1982, pp.608–18; P. Blackwell and J. Gessner, 'Fear and trembling; an inquiry into adolescent perspectives of living in a nuclear age', *Youth and Society*, vol.15, 1983, pp.238–55.
23 C. Lasch, *The Culture of Narcissism*, London, Abacus, 1980; *The Minimal Self*, London, Picador, 1984.
24 Also see J. Dunn, *Western Political Theory in the Face of the Future*, Cambridge, Cambridge University Press, 1979, especially p.78.
25 R. Sennett, *The Fall of Public Man*, Cambridge, Cambridge University Press, 1977, p.34.
26 A.R. Hochschild. *The Managed Heart: Commercialization of Human Feeling*, London, University of California Press, 1983.
27 This was essentially Darwin's view in *The Expression of Emotions in Man and Animals*, New York, Philosophical Library, 1955 (1872), which Hochschild sees as a still powerful model.
28 Giddens, 1984, op. cit., pp.28–34.
29 For instance H. Ornauer *et al.* (eds), *Images of the World in the Year 2000*, The Hague, Mouton, 1976. This was a survey of 11,000 individuals in fourteen countries which posed exactly this methodological problem.
30 H.H. Davis, *Beyond Class Images*, London, Croom Helm, 1979.
31 For instance, A. Touraine, *La Conscience Ouvrière*, Paris, Editions du Seuil, 1966; J.H. Goldthorpe *et al.*, *The Affluent Worker: Political Attitudes and Behaviour*, Cambridge, Cambridge University Press, 1968; M. Bulmer (ed.), *Working Class Images of Society*, London, Routledge & Kegan Paul, 1975.
32 Davis, op. cit., p.31.
33 A. Willener, *The Action-Image of Society*, London, Tavistock, 1970.
34 M. Emmison, 'Class images of the economy; an empirical examination

of opposition and incorporation within working class consciousness', *Sociology*, vol.19, no.1, 1985, pp.19–38.
35 C.W. Mills, 'Situated actions and vocabularies of motive' in I.L. Horowitz (ed.), *Power, Politics and People, the Collected Essays of C. Wright Mills*, London, Oxford University Press, 1967.
36 Especially in A. Touraine, *Anti-Nuclear Protest*, Cambridge, Cambridge University Press, 1983.

CHAPTER 3 THE CONCEPT OF PESSIMISM

1 On the importance and unavoidability of time see H. Martins, 'Time and theory in sociology', in J. Rex (ed.), *Approaches to Sociology*, London, Routledge & Kegan Paul, 1974
2 See J. Bailey, *Ideas and Intervention*, London, Routledge & Kegan Paul, 1980, ch.6.
3 On the significance of etymology for sociologists see R. Williams, *Keywords: a Vocabulary of Culture and Society*, London, Fontana, 1976.
4 L. Loemker, 'Pessimism', in *Encyclopaedia of Philosophy*, New York, Collier-Macmillan, 1967.
5 In spite of Voltaire's satire on optimism in *Candide*. The term was first popularly used by Coleridge.
6 J. Monod, *Chance and Necessity; An Essay on the Natural Philosophy of Modern Biology*, London, Collins, 1972, pp.20,31.
7 L. Tiger, *Optimism: the Biology of Hope*, New York, Simon and Schuster, 1979.
8 B. Russell, *The History of Western Philosophy*, London, George Allen & Unwin, 1979 (1946), p.727.
9 For an interesting pursuit of the implications of these philosophical positions for social thought see J. Goudsblom, *Nihilism and Culture*, Oxford, Blackwell, 1980.
10 J.J. Clarke, 'Sunt Lacrimae Rerum: a study in the logic of pessimism', *Philosophy*, vol.XLV, no.173, pp.193–209.
11 By for instance A.J. Ayer, *The Problems of Knowledge*, Harmondsworth, Penguin, 1956.
12 F. Kermode, *The Sense of an Ending: Studies in the Theory of Fiction*, Oxford, Oxford University Press, 1967,
13 E. Gellner, 'Our current sense of history', *Archives Européennes de Sociologie*, vol.X11, no.2, 1971, pp.159–82.
14 J. Passmore, *The Perfectibility of Man*, London, Duckworth, 1970.
15 This begs a number of questions raised first by Durkheim about the *inherently* overweening potential of human nature. See R.A. Nisbet, *The Sociological Tradition*, London, Heinemann, 1967, pp.150–61.

16 J.A. Beckford, *Cult Controversies; the Social Response to the New Religious Movements*, London, Tavistock, 1985.

17 For example see C. Lasch, *The Minimal Self*, London, Picador, 1984; S. Bellow and M. Amis, 'Our valuation of human life has become thinner', *Listener*, 13 March 1986. This was one of a series of interviews/conversations called 'Modernity and its Discontents' which was notably pessimistic.

18 E.P. Thompson, 'Notes on Exterminism, the Last Stage of Civilisation', *New Left Review*, no.121, 1980, pp.3–27.

19 F.L. Baumer, 'Twentieth century versions of the apocalypse', *Cahiers d'Histoire Mondiale*, vol.1, no.3,1954, pp.623–40; F. Polak, *The Image of the Future*, Amsterdam, Elsevier, 1973 (1954).

20 G. Steiner, *In Bluebeard's Castle*, London, Faber, 1971.

21 W.W. Wagar, *Glad Tidings; The Belief in Progress from Darwin to Marcuse*, Bloomington Ind., Indiana University Press, 1972; *Terminal Visions: the Literature of Last Things*, Bloomington Ind., Indiana University Press, 1983.

22 A. Giddens, *Central Problems in Social Theory*, London, Macmillan, 1979, pp.245–6.

23 A. Gouldner, *The Coming Crisis of Western Sociology*, London, Heinemann, 1971, ch.2.

24 T. Parsons, *The Social System*, London, Routledge & Kegan Paul, London, 1951, pp.11–13.

25 L. Sklair, *The Sociology of Progress*, London, Routledge & Kegan Paul, 1970, chs.V,VI.

26 H. Vyverberg, *Historical Pessimism in the French Enlightenment*, Cambridge Mass., Harvard University Press, 1958.

27 Nisbet, 1967, op. cit., p.256.

28 E. Durkheim, *The Division of Labour in Society*, New York, Free Press, 1964 (1893), pp.401–2.

29 H.S. Hughes, *Consciousness in Society*, London, McGibbon and Kee, 1967, pp.287–90.

30 We can select our founding fathers to provide a darker vision. Pareto's and Freud's different but equally dismal views of the dominance of the non-rational might provide an alternative Pantheon along with Toqueville, Nietzsche and Schopenhauer.

31 See L. Coser, 'American Trends' in T. Bottomore and R. Nisbet (eds), *A History of Sociological Analysis*, London, Heinemann, 1978; G. Hawthorne, *Enlightenment and Despair*, Cambridge, Cambridge University Press, 1976.

32 M. Levy Jr., *The Structure of Society*, Princeton NJ., Princeton University Press, 1952.

33 Hawthorne, 1976, op. cit., ch.8; P. Abrams, *The Origins of British Sociology*, Harmondsworth, Penguin, 1968.

34   Perhaps the totemic statement of this period is Gouldner's essay on
     'Metaphysical Pathos and the Theory of Bureaucracy', *American
     Political Science Review*, vol.49, 1955, pp.496–507. It has a clear view of
     the pessimism implicit in organisation theory which is neutralised by
     Gouldner's concern that social scientists tell how men might mitigate
     and control bureaucracy. Gouldner confronts the gloomy side of Weber
     and slickly upends it into a lesson for lagging optimists. Also see A.
     Sicinski, 'Optimism versus pessimism; tentative concepts and their
     consequences for future research', *The Polish Sociological Bulletin*,
     vol.25–6, no.1–2, pp.47–62; L.M. Killian, 'Optimism and pessimism
     in sociological analysis', *American Sociologist*, vol.6, no.4, 1971,
     pp.281–6.
35   For instance J. Urry, 'Sociology as a parasite; some uses and unities', in
     P. Abrams *et al*. (eds), *Practice and Progress: British Sociology 1950–
     1980*, London, George Allen & Unwin, 1981.
36   C.W. Mills, *The Sociological Imagination*, London, Oxford University
     Press, 1956.
37   P. Abrams, 'The collapse of British sociology?', in Abrams *et al*. (eds),
     1981, op. cit.
38   E. Etzioni–Halevy, *The Knowledge Elite and the Future of Prophecy*,
     London, George Allen & Unwin, 1985, p.52.
39   W. Lepenies, 'Cold reason and the culture of the feelings; social
     science, literature and the end of the Enlightenment', *Social Science
     Information*, vol.24, no.1, 1985, pp.3–21.
40   The period after the mid–1960s was marked by the eclipse, at least in
     the universities of the literary and 'high culture' intellectuals by the
     newly apparent and numerous social scientists and especially the
     sociologists. Malcolm Bradbury's bitter and funny novel *The History
     Man*, London, Secker and Warburg, 1975, is both a description and a
     satire of their claims to superiority.
41   W. Lepenies, 'The critique of learning and science and the crisis of
     orientation', *Social Science Information*, vol.19, no.1, 1980, pp.1–37.
42   R.B. Bailey III, *Sociology Faces Pessimism: A Study of European
     Sociological Thought Amidst a Fading Optimism*, The Hague, Martinus
     Nijhoff, 1958.

CHAPTER 4 THE END OF PROGRESS

1   For 'need' see M. Ignatieff, *The Needs of Strangers*, London, Chatto and
    Windus, 1984.
2   See R. Williams, *Keywords*, London, Fontana, 1976, the entry on
    'Progressive' for the development of meaning.

3 R. Aronson, *The Dialectics of Disaster: A Preface to Hope*, London, Verso, 1983, p.14, provides a brief 'inventory of death'.
4 H. Ornauer *et al.* (eds), *Images of the World in the Year 2000*, The Hague, Mouton, 1976.
5 H-U. Kohr and H-G. Rader (eds), *New Social Movements and the Perception of Military Threat in Western Democracies*, Munich, Sozialwissentschaftliches Institut der Bundeswehr, Forum 3, 1983; 'Generational Learning, Moral Judgement and Military Threat', paper presented to the annual conference of the British Sociological Association, University of Hull, 1985. See chapter 8.
6 See especially S.B. Withey and F.M. Andrews, *Social Indicators of Well-Being*, New York, Plenum Press, 1977. For focused data on attitude change see H. Meulemann, 'Value change in West Germany', *Social Science Information*, vol.22, nos.4–5, 1983, pp.777–800.
7 J. Dunn, *Western Political Theory in the Face of the Future*, Cambridge, Cambridge University Press, 1979, p.30.
8 For instance many of the contributors to G. Almond, M. Chodorow and R.H. Pearce (eds), *Progress and its Discontents*, Berkeley Cal., University of California Press, 1982.
9 S.H. Barnes, 'Changing popular attitudes to progress' in G. Almond *et al.* (eds), op. cit. This is based on Maslow's well known 'Hierarchy of needs'.
10 See chapter 9 for some of the evidence.
11 *Events* are highly visible but have a problematic relation to *processes*. The latter are what social scientists focus on but we need to explain how events are manifestations or products – or not – of them.
12 For an interesting account of the relation in practice see P. Wright, *On Living in an Old Country*, London, Verso, 1985.
13 Cynicism is a much ignored form of consciousness. See P. Sloterdijk, 'Cynicism: the twilight of false-consciousness', *New German Critique*, vol.33, 1984, pp.190–4.
14 R. Williams, *Towards 2000*, London, Chatto and Windus, 1983, pp.190–4.
15 There are a number of excellent histories of the concept of progress. See particularly and contrastingly K. Kumar, *Prophecy and Progress*, Harmondsworth, Penguin, 1978; R. Nisbet, *History of the Idea of Progress*, New York, Basic Books, 1980.
16 G. Hawthorne, *Enlightenment and Despair*, Cambridge, Cambridge University Press, 1976.
17 H. Vyverberg, *Historical Pessimism in the French Enlightenment*, Cambridge Mass., Harvard University Press, 1958.
18 J. Bailey, *Social Theory for Planning*, London, Routledge & Kegan Paul, 1975, ch.3.
19 L. Sklair, *The Sociology of Progress*, London, Routledge & Kegan Paul, 1970, pp.63–4.

20 See chapter 5.
21 Sklair, 1970, op. cit., ch.VIII.
22 Nisbet, 1980, op. cit. This individualism dominates utilitarianism then and now.
23 For the best known statement about the increasing centrality of knowledge see D. Bell, *The Coming of Post-Industrial Society*, Harmondsworth, Penguin, 1976, ch.3.
24 A. Smith, *Wealth of Nations*, London, Dent, 1910.
25 H.W. Arndt, *The Rise and Fall of Economic Growth*, Melbourne, Longman Cheshire Pty., 1979.
26 Bell, 1976, op. cit., pp.196–212.
27 M.J. Wiener, *English Culture and the Decline of the Industrial Spirit 1850–1980*, Cambridge, Cambridge University Press, 1980, has had a powerful effect on Conservative politicians.
28 F. Hirsch, *Social Limits to Growth*, London, Routledge & Kegan Paul, 1977. For a commentary see A. Ellis and K. Kumar (eds), *Dilemmas of Liberal Democracies: Studies in Fred Hirsch's Social Limits to Growth*, London, Tavistock, 1983.
29 For instance E.J. Mishan, *The Costs of Economic Growth*, London, Staples Press, 1967; T. Roszak, *Where the Wasteland Ends: Politics and Transcendance in Post-Industrial Society*, New York, Doubleday, 1970; I. Illich, *The Right to Useful Employment*, London, Boyars, 1978.
30 For instance I. Miles and J. Irvine (eds), *The Poverty of Progress: Changing Ways of Life in Industrial Societies*, Oxford, Pergamon, 1983; E. Masini (ed.), *Visions of Desirable Societies*, Oxford, Pergamon, 1983.
31 Aronson, 1983, op. cit., p.193.
32 This moderates the argument by Popper and Hayek, among others, who argue the necessarily authoritarian character of social planning. See chapter 5.
33 See chapter 9.
34 For instance H. Kahn and J. Wiener, *The Year 2000*, London, Macmillan, 1967.
35 Chapter 6 deals with the recent products of futurology in more detail but for an overall classification see S. Cole, 'The Global Futures Debate, 1965–76', in C. Freeman and M. Jahoda (eds), *World Futures: The Great Debate*, London, Martin Robertson, 1978.
36 J. Forester, *World Dynamics*, Cambridge Mass., Wright–Allen, 1971; D. Meadows *et al.*, *The Limits to Growth*, New York, Universe Books, 1972.
37 E. Rothschild, 'How Doomed are We?', *New York Review of Books*, vol.XXII, no.11, pp.31–4.
38 V. Ferkiss, 'The pessimistic outlook' in J. Fowles (ed.), *Handbook of Futures Research*, Westpoint, Conn., Greenwood Press, 1978.
39 As was made clear in some of the best responses such as I. Miles, *The Poverty of Prediction*, Farnborough, Saxon House, 1975; Science Policy

Research Unit, 'The Limits to Growth Controversy', *Futures*, 5, 1975, whole issue.
40 Particularly R. Heilbroner, *An Inquiry into the Human Prospect*, London, Calder, 1975.

CHAPTER 5 UTOPIAS

1 B. Goodwin and K. Taylor, *The Politics of Utopia: A Study in Theory and Practice*, London, Hutchinson, 1982 has an excellent bibliography. F. and F. Manuel, *Utopian Thought in the Western World*, Oxford, Balckwell, 1979 is a detailed historical account.
2 R. Levitas, 'Sociology and Utopia', *Sociology*, vol.13, no.1, 1979, pp.19–33 is a useful conceptual overview of utopia as a mode of thought and attempts to provide an analytic perspective; B. Goodwin, *Social Science and Utopias*, Sussex, Harvester, 1978, treats utopians as soi-disant social scientists and utopias as models of functioning societies.
3 Its literary form is well known. Some of the most profound and popular writings of our time are in a utopian (or dystopian) form – Orwell, Huxley and now, increasingly science fiction and feminist novels. From a large secondary literature see I.F. Clarke, *The Pattern of Expectation; 1644–2001*, London, Cape, 1979.
4 Goodwin and Taylor, 1982, op. cit., pp.207–10 attempt to deal with this issue which is profoundly problematic in all utilitarian conceptions of welfare and, recently, notably in the work of J. Rawls, *A Theory of Justice*, Harvard Mass., Harvard University Press, 1971.
5 The criticism of the socialist utopia in Z. Bauman, *Socialism: The Active Utopia*, London, Allen & Unwin, 1976 is the best example. But we could also consider small scale communitarianism: see R. Kanter, *Commitment and Community: Communes and Utopias in Sociological Perspective*, Harvard Mass., Harvard University Press, 1972. Explicit utopianising as a practical speculation seems feeble too; see E. Masini (ed.), *Visions of Desirable Societies*, Oxford, Pergamon, 1983; R. Bahro, *The Alternative in Eastern Europe*, London, New Left Books, 1978.
6 F. Manuel (ed.) *Utopias and Utopian Thought*, New York, Souvenir Press, 1973.
7 For instance Levitas, 1979, op. cit.
8 K. Mannheim, *Ideology and Utopia*, London, Routledge & Kegan Paul, 1960 (1936).
9 R. Williams, *Towards 2000*, London, Chatto and Windus, 1983, pp.12–14.
10 Goodwin and Taylor, 1982, op. cit., p.58.
11 See Clarke, op. cit., 1979 for examples of this distinction in practice.

12   See R. Williams, 'Utopia and Science Fiction', *Science Fiction Studies*, vol.5, no.3, 1978, pp.196–212.
13   Goodwin and Taylor, 1982, op. cit., p.47 note that Edward Bellamy's *Looking Backward 2000–1887*, 1888, was probably the most widely read fiction of any. Ebenezer Howard's *Garden Cities of Tomorrow*, 1898, was also exceptionally popular.
14   For instance C. Brinton, 'Utopia and Democracy' in F. Manuel (ed.) 1979, op. cit.
15   Notably Bauman, 1976, op. cit.; but also G. Lichtheim, *Marxism*, London, Routledge & Kegan Paul, 1967; E. Kamenka, *The Ethical Foundations of Marxism*, London, Routledge & Kegan Paul, 1972.
16   Mannheim, 1960, op. cit.
17   Goodwin, 1978, op. cit.
18   Bahro, 1978, op. cit., p.263.
19   Most forcefully – and scornfully – in D. Selbourne, *Against Socialist Illusion*, London, Macmillan, 1985.
20   K. Popper, *The Open Society and Its Enemies*, London, Routledge & Kegan Paul, 1945; *Conjectures and Refutations*, London, Routledge & Kegan Paul, 1963, chs.16–18.
21   C.F. Alford, 'Critical rationalism and the problem of utopia', *Polity*, vol.14, no.3, 1981–2, pp.481–500.
22   As, importantly, in Rawls, 1971, op. cit., but also, ironically, in Habermas' notion of 'the ideal speech situation'; see chapter 2 note 12.
23   G. Kateb, *Utopia and its Enemies*, New York, Collier-Macmillan, 1963.
24   Popper, 1945, op. cit., vol.1, pp.161–2.
25   F. Hayek, *The Road to Serfdom*, London, Routledge & Kegan Paul, London, 1962 (1944); *Law, Legislation and Liberty*, London, Routledge & Kegan Paul, 1977, 3 vols.; J. Davis, *Utopia and the Ideal Society*, Cambridge, Cambridge University Press, 1981.
26   See Goodwin and Taylor, 1982, op. cit., p.97 for an expansion of this point.
27   See Popper, 1945, op. cit., vol.1, p.288 note 7.
28   Selbourne, 1985, op. cit.
29   Ibid., p.229.
30   Ibid., p.232–3.
31   Ibid., p.217.
32   Though an inaccurate one. The utopian mode of thought is alive and well and living on in the 'new politics' – see chapter 9 – in new fictional artistic forms, especially in science fiction literature and films, and in particular forms of conventional politics – as developed later in this chapter.
33   F. Kermode, *The Sense of an Ending: Studies in the Theory of Fiction*, Oxford, Oxford University Press, 1967; W.W. Wagar, *Terminal Visions: the Literature of Last Things*, Bloomington Ind., Bloomington University Press, 1983.

34 G. Steiner, *In Bluebeard's Castle*, London, Faber, 1971, p.73.
35 Williams, 1978, op. cit.
36 Bauman, 1976, op. cit., ch.2.
37 E.P. Thompson, *William Morris: Romantic to Revolutionary*, London, Merlin, 1977. Also see P. Anderson, *Arguments Within English Socialism*, London, Verso, 1980, ch.6, 'Utopias'; R. Williams, *The Long Revolution*, Harmondsworth, Penguin, 1965, pp.153–61.
38 See generally R. Levitas (ed.), *The Ideology of the New Right*, Cambridge, Cambridge University Press, 1986; N. Bosanquet, *After the New Right*, London, Heinemann, 1983.
39 Levitas, 1986, op. cit., pp.91–3.
40 The 'Omega Reports', published by the Adam Smith Institute, are a series of detailed policy and planning reports which set out the practical implications of new right views for most public policy areas. See R. Levitas, 'Competition and compliance: the utopias of the new right' in Levitas (ed.), 1986, op. cit.
41 Mannheim, 1960, op. cit., pp.210–11.
42 Williams, 1983, op. cit., p.133; *Television; Technology and Cultural Form*, London, Fontana, 1974.
43 For instance D. Michie and R. Johnston, *The Creative Computer: Machine Intelligence and Human Knowledge*, Harmondsworth, Penguin, 1985; P. Jenkin, 'Automation is good for us', in T. Forester (ed.), *The Information Technology Revolution*, Oxford, Blackwell, 1985; H. A Simon, 'What computers mean for man and society', in T. Forester (ed.), *The Microelectronics Revolution*, Oxford, Blackwell, 1982.
44 E.P. Thompson (ed.), *Star Wars*, Harmondsworth, Penguin, 1985.
45 J. Gershuny, *After Industrial Society*, London, Macmillan, 1978, ch.1.
46 See K. Kumar, 'Thoughts on the present discontents in Britain', *Theory and Society*, vol.9, 1980, pp.539–74 for a comment on the relevance of this group now.
47 D. Bell, *The Coming of Post-Industrial Society*, Harmondsworth, Penguin, 1976.
48 Ibid., pp.109,298.
49 Especially K. Kumar, *Prophecy and Progress*, Harmondsworth, Penguin, 1978; Gershuny, 1978, op. cit.; J. Hall, *Diagnoses of Our Time: Six Views of our Social Condition*, London, Heinemann, 1981, pp.103–14.
50 I. Clarke, 'World order reform and utopian thought: a contemporary watershed', *Review of Politics*, vol.41, no.1, 1979, pp.96–120.

CHAPTER 6 FUTURES

1 Rather than the reverse. For an interesting discussion of the analytic dimensions of forecasting see D. Bell, *The Coming of Post-Industrial Society*, Harmondsworth, Penguin, 1976, pp.1–33.

2 Most general treatments of forecasting give useful bibliographies which are really summary histories of the genre. See K. Kumar, *Prophecy and Progress*, Harmondsworth, Penguin, 1978, pp.355–6 notes 2–6.

3 For alternative classifications of *kinds* of forecasting see S. Cole, 'The global futures debate, 1965–76' in C. Freeman and M. Jahoda (eds), *World Futures; The Great Debate*, London, Martin Robertson, 1978.

4 For examples of these changing meanings in practice see C. Bailey, *A Loving Conspiracy*, London, Quartet, 1984.

5 On the significance of 'images' of the future see I. Miles, S. Cole and J. Gershuny, 'Images of the Future' in Freeman and Jahoda (eds) 1978, op. cit.; E. Boulding, 'Futuristics and the imaging capacity of the west' in M. Maruyama and J. Dator (eds), *Human Futuristics*, Honolulu Hawaii, University of Hawaii, 1971; B.J. Huber, 'Imaging the future' in J. Fowles (ed.), *Handbook of Futures Research*, Westpoint, Conn., Greenwood Press, 1978. The *locus classicus* is F. Polak, *The Image of the Future*, Amsterdam, Elsevier, 1973 (1954). This is a rather different idea of 'image' to that proposed in chapter 2.

6 J. Forester, *World Dynamics*, Cambridge Mass., Wright–Allen, 1971; D. Meadows *et al.*, *The Limits to Growth*, New York, Universe Books, 1972.

7 M. Mesarovic and E. Pestel, *Mankind at the Turning Point*, New York, Dutton, 1974.

8 The Club of Rome was an international group of 'elite' academics, public officials, politicians and businessmen the aim of which was to alert political leaders to the interacting problems of the environment, population and resource use.

9 E. Rothschild, 'How Doomed Are We?', *New York Review of Books*, vol.XXII, no.11, 1975, pp.31–4.

10 Science Policy Research Unit, 'The Limits to Growth Controversy', *Futures* vol.5, 1975, whole issue; I. Miles, *The Poverty of Prediction*, Farnborough, Saxon House, 1975.

11 W. Beckerman, *Two Cheers for the Affluent Society*, London, St Martin's Press, 1975.

12 Notably in the works of H. Kahn, for instance, 'Things are going rather well', *Futurist*, vol.IX, no.6, 1975, pp.290–2; *The Coming Boom, Economic, Political and Social*, London, Hutchinson, 1983.

13 For instance J.L. Simon and H. Kahn (eds), *The Resourceful Earth, A Response to Global 2000*, Oxford, Blackwell, 1984.

14 Interestingly by R. Williams, *Towards 2000*, London, Chatto and

Windus, 1983; J. Ferkiss, 'Pessimism about the future; a new departure or return to normal?', *Alternative Futures*, vol.3, no.3, 1980, pp.111–25.

15 Global 2000, *Report to the President of the U.S.: Entering the 21st. Century*, Oxford, Pergamon, 1980, vol.1, Summary Report.

16 Simon and Kahn, (eds), 1984, op. cit.

17 Ibid., p.6.

18 H Kahn and J. Wiener, *The Year 2000*, London, Macmillan, 1967.

19 For instance Miles, 1975, op. cit. G. Myrdal, *Against the Stream*, New York, Vintage Books, 1975, p.201 refers to it as 'quasi-learnedness'.

20 J. Bailey, *Social Theory for Planning*, London, Routledge & Kegan Paul, 1975, ch.4.

21 R. Heilbroner, *An Inquiry into the Human Prospect*, London, Calder, 1975.

22 Williams, 1983, op. cit., pp.6–10.

23 Rothschild, 1975, op. cit..

24 Simon and Kahn (eds), 1984, op. cit., especially p.46.

25 For instances R.J. Johnston and P.J. Taylor (eds), *A World in Crisis?*, Oxford, Blackwell, 1986.

26 For instance J. Galtung, *Environment, Development and Military Activity*, Oslo, Universitetsforlaget, 1982.

27 E. Masini (ed.), *Visions of Desirable Societies*, Oxford, Pergamon, 1983.

28 Boulding, 1971, op. cit.

29 F. Polak, 1973, op. cit. Also see his *Prognostics: A Science in the Making Surveys the Future*, Amsterdam, Elsevier, 1981.

30 Simon and Kahn (eds), 1984, op. cit., pp.3–6; Kahn, 1983, op. cit., pp.45–8.

31 But see A. Giddens, *Central Problems in Social Theory*, London, Macmillan, 1979, ch.6.

32 See H. Martins, 'Time and theory in sociology', in J. Rex (ed.), *Approaches to Sociology*, London, Routledge & Kegan Paul, 1974 to see how difficult.

33 Ibid.

34 D. Rowe, *Living with the Bomb*, London, Routledge & Kegan Paul, 1985; R. Aronson, *The Dialectics of Disaster: A Preface to Hope*, London, Verso, 1983.

35 B. Tuchman, *A Distant Mirror: The Calamitous 14th Century*, Harmondsworth, Penguin, 1979, pp.103–5, 121–5.

36 For an account of 'pluritemporalism' see Martins, 1974, op. cit., pp.266–9.

37 F. Kermode, *The Sense of an Ending: Studies in the Theory of Fiction*, Oxford, Oxford University Press, 1967 – particularly on 'naive apocalypticism'. Also see Williams, 1983, op. cit., pp.3–5.

38 E. Gellner, 'Our current sense of history', *Archives Européennes de Sociologie*, vol. XII, no.2, 1971, pp.159–82. The current interest in

'waves' of social change, in sequential 'repetition' is a version of this interest.

39 'as if society was on the verge of, or perhaps even in the first phase of, some kind of vast social or cultural revolution whose exact nature has not yet been understood but of which people see premonitions all around them'. H. Simmons, 'Systems dynamics and technocracy' in Science Policy Research Unit, 1973, op. cit.

40 Johnston and Taylor (eds) 1986, op. cit., p.1.

41 As Kahn, 1983, op. cit., pp.44–5, would have it and, indeed, Bell, 1976, op. cit., pp.487–9.

42 Polak, 1973, op. cit., p.152. The comments were directed at Popper.

43 Williams, 1983, op. cit., pp.260–9.

44 I. Miles and J. Irvine (eds), *The Poverty of Progress*, Oxford, Pergamon, 1983.

CHAPTER 7 THE MAIN DANGER: NUCLEAR WAR

1 There are gross difficulties in assessing public opinion as such basic attitudes and feelings. The very nature of the aggregate of individual views, gathered by surveyors and pollsters, makes this sort of data only one relevant indication of the state of 'culture'.

2 C. Lasch, *The Minimal Self*, London, Picador, 1984, pp.60–4.

3 A. Mazur, 'Disputes between experts', *Minerva*, vol.XI, No.2, 1973, pp.243–62; D. Nelkin (ed.), *Controversy: the Politics of Technical Decisions*, London, Sage, 1979; J. Krige, 'The politics of truth' in N. Blake and K. Pole (eds), *Objections to Nuclear Defence: Philosophers on Deterrence*, London, Routledge & Kegan Paul, 1984.

4 See D. Gross, 'Left melancholy', *Telos*, vol.65, 1985, pp.112–21.

5 But see R.C. Kramer and S. Marullo, 'Towards a sociology of nuclear weapons', *Sociological Quarterly*, vol.26, no.3, 1985, pp.277–92 which has a useful bibliography of specifically sociological contributions.

6 The numerous publications and activities of SANA (Scientists Against Nuclear Arms), for instance SANA, *The Nuclear Balance*, Milton Keynes, SANA, 1984; IPPNW (International Physicians for the Prevention of Nuclear War), *Last Aid*, London 1983.

7 For instance see M. Shaw (ed.), *War, State and Society*, London, Macmillan, 1984.

8 As given in G. Rumble, *The Politics of Nuclear Defence: A Comprehensive Introduction*, Cambridge, Polity Press, 1985, ch.6.

9 Notable fictional attempts are A–A. Guha, *Ende: Diary of the Third World War*, London, Corgi, 1986; W. Strieber and J. Kunetka, *Warday and the Journey Onward*, London, Hodder and Stoughton, 1984; R. Hoban, *Riddley Walker*, London, Cape, 1980, is an attempt to describe

a post-nuclear world, centuries after the catastrophe. R. Briggs, *When the Wind Blows*, London, Hamish Hamilton, 1982, was a powerful cartoon story which was adapted as a radio and stage play, and a full-length cartoon feature film.

10 C. Sagan, 'Nuclear war and climatic catastrophe: some policy implications', *Foreign Affairs*, vol.62, no.2, 1983, pp.257–92; 'Nuclear winter: a report for the world scientific community', *Environment*, vol.27, no.8, 1985, pp.12–15; O. Greene, I. Percival and I. Ridge, *Nuclear Winter*, Cambridge, Polity Press, 1985.

11 Counting the number of warheads is only one, very imperfect, way of assessing the destructive potential. In 1984 there was a total of about 19,000 strategic warheads controlled by the US and the USSR; see Rumble, 1985, op. cit., p.29 table 2.5; also see SANA, 1984, op. cit.

12 This is the burden of J. Schell, *The Abolition*, London, Cape, 1984.

13 There are some impressively thorough attempts to estimate the effects of nuclear war which cast measured doubt on official civil defence positions. One of the best is P. Clarke, *London Under Attack: Report of the Greater London Area War Risk Commission (GLAWARS)*, Oxford, Blackwell, 1986. Also see D. Campbell, *War Plan UK: the Truth About Civil Defence in Britain*, London, Burnett Books, 1982. Rumble, 1985, op. cit. provides a partial summary of evidence up to 1985.

14 A.M. Katz, *Life After Nuclear War: The Economic and Social Impacts of Nuclear Attacks on the US*, Cambridge Mass., Ballinger Publishing Company. The study was in fact conducted in 1979.

15 See note 9. This is especially true of Guha's short book which was originally published in West Germany where the sense of the immediacy of the threat is high.

16 E.P. Thompson, 'Notes on exterminism, the last stage of civilisation', *New Left Review*, no.121, 1980, pp.3–27. Also see R. Williams, *Towards 2000*, London, Chatto and Windus, 1983, pp.220–2, for a sympathetic account.

17 S. Zuckerman, *Nuclear Illusion and Reality*, London, Collins, 1982; *Science Advisers, Scientific Advisers and Nuclear Weapons*, London, Menard Press, 1981; Zuckerman has made penetrating comments on developments in strategic doctrine and weaponry particularly in a number of book review articles in the *New York Review of Books* between 1983 and 1985.

18 See for example W.J. Broad, *Star Warriors: A Penetrating Look into the Lives of the Young Scientists Behind our Space Age Weaponry*, New York, Simon and Schuster, 1985.

19 See B. Easlea, *Fathering the Unthinkable: Masculinity, Scientists and the Nuclear Arms Race*, London, Pluto Press, 1983. He says there is a masculine antipathy to simple, logical solutions to scientific problems and a premium on risk, hazard, complexity and difficulty. There is 'a compulsive desire to lord it over other people and non-human nature

and then manfully to confront a dangerous world'. p.165.
20 But, as an important exception, see M. Kaldor, *The Baroque Arsenal*, London, Deutsch, 1982.
21 Broad, 1982, op. cit.; one interviewee described his colleagues at the Livermore Laboratory, which is a leading edge weapons research organisation, as 'socially maladjusted'.
22 This is the crucial fantasy in the original speech by President Reagan delivered on 23 March 1983 announcing SDI.
23 D. Ford, *The Button: the Pentagon's Strategic Command and Control System*, New York, Simon & Schuster, 1985; P. Bracken, *The Command and Control of Nuclear Forces*, Yale Conn., Yale University Press, 1984.
24 D. Frei, *Risks of Unintentional Nuclear War*, Geneva, UNIDIR, 1982, p.17.
25 Kaldor, 1982, op. cit., especially p.220.
26 G. Adams, *The Iron Triangle: the Politics of Defense Contracting*, New York, Council on Economic Priorities, 1981; S. Lens, *The Military-Industrial Complex*, London, Stanmore Press, 1971.
27 See SIPRI, *Yearbooks of World Armaments and Disarmament*, London, Taylor and Francis, yearly.
28 Thompson (ed.), 1985, op. cit., pp.120–1; 'Weapons in Space', *Daedelus*, vol.114, nos.2 and 3, 1985.
29 In Britain defence-related expenditure generally grew by 25 per cent in real terms between 1979 and 1984, total public expenditure by only 7 per cent. In 1982 about 5 per cent of British public R & D expenditure went to military projects. Twenty per cent of British electronics industry output and 45 per cent of the output of the aerospace industry were weapons connected, see J. Simmie and N. James, 'The money map of defence', *New Society*, 31 January, 1986, pp.179–80; N. Ball and M. Leitenberg, *The Structure of the Defence Industry*, London, Croom Helm, 1982.
30 T. Draper, 'Nuclear Temptations', *New York Review of Books*, vol.XXX, no.21, 1984, pp.42–50.
31 A good survey is, again, in Rumble, 1985, op. cit., ch.3.
32 Respectively, V.D. Sokolovskii (ed.), *Military Strategy*, Moscow, Military Publishing House, 1968 (3rd. edition), quoted in Zuckerman, 1982, op. cit., p.73; H. Schmidt, *Defense or Retaliation*, New York, Praeger; R.S. McNamara, 'The military role of nuclear weapons: perceptions and misperceptions', *Foreign Affairs*, vol.62, no.1, 1983, pp.59–80.
33 Draper, 1984, op. cit.
34 R. Scheer, *With Enough Shovels: Reagan, Bush and Nuclear War*, London, Secker and Warburg, 1982.
35 See S. Marullo, 'The ideological nature of nuclear deterrence: some causes and consequences', *Sociological Quarterly*, vol.26, no.3, 1985,

pp.311–30; and also many of the contributions to Blake and Pole (eds), 1984, op. cit.

36 This is the position of Zuckerman, Draper and Freeman among many others.

37 R. Aronson, *The Dialectics of Disaster: A Preface to Hope*, London, Verso, 1983, pp.193–7.

38 See the criticism of J. Schell, *The Fate of the Earth*, London, Picador, 1982; by S. Zuckerman, 'Nuclear Fantasies', *New York Review of Books*, vol.XXXI, no.10, 1984, pp.5–12.

39 J. Thompson, *Psychological Aspects of Nuclear War*, Chichester, British Psychological Society/Wiley, 1985.

40 See chapter 2, note 22.

41 R.J. Lifton, 'Imagining the real: beyond the nuclear end', in L. Grinspoon (ed.), *The Long Darkness: Psychological and Moral Perspectives on Nuclear Winter*, Yale, Yale University Press, 1986.

42 K. Soper, 'Human survival', in Blake and Pole (eds), 1984, op. cit., p.92.

43 For instance see J.D. Frank, 'Pre-nuclear age leaders and the nuclear arms race', *American Journal of Ortho-Psychiatry*, vol.52, 1982, pp.132–7.

44 See S. Zuckerman, 1982, op. cit., pp.142–3: namely; 1 1950, Truman in Korea after the retreat from Yalu – he was dissuaded by Attlee. 2 Eisenhower to raise the siege of Dien Bien Phu in Vietnam – he was dissuaded by Churchill. 3 Nixon to raise the siege of Khe Sanh in Vietnam. Who dissuaded him?

45 For instance K.F. Otterbein, *The Evolution of War: A Cross-Cultural Study*, New Haven, Conn., Human Relations Area Files Press, 1970.

46 Easlea, 1983, op. cit.

47 For instance M. Kidron, *Western Capitalism since the War*, London, Weidenfeld and Nicolson, 1968.

CHAPTER 8 MORE DANGERS: FOOD AND NUCLEAR ENERGY

1 S. Cotgrove, *Catastrophe or Cornucopia*, Chichester, Wiley, 1982.

2 See for instance, L. Milbrath, *Environmentalists: Vanguard for a New Society*, Albany New York, State University of New York Press, 1984.

3 An economistic and managerial approach emphasises this, for instance J. Levihan and W.W. Fletcher (eds), *Economics of the Environment*, New York, Academic Press, 1979.

4 T.C. Sinclair, 'Environmentalism', in Science Policy Research Unit, 'The Limits to Growth Controversy', *Futures*, vol.5, 1973.

5   Milbrath, 1984, op. cit.; F. Sandbach, *Environment, Ideology and Policy*, Oxford, Blackwell, 1980.

6   Cotgrove, 1982, op. cit., pp.12–18 for public opinion. It may be that some events 'burst through' social processes – such as Chernobyl?

7   See B. Moore Jr, *Reflections on the Causes of Human Misery*, London, Allen Lane, 1972; J. Bailey, *Ideas and Intervention*, London, Routledge & Kegan Paul, 1980, pp.13–14.

8   For an earlier optimist see J. Maddox, *The Doomsday Syndrome*, London, Macmillan, 1972. For a slightly later example see M.W. Holdgate, *A Perspective of Environmental Pollution*, Cambridge, Cambridge University Press, 1979, especially ch.10.

9   See C.C. Park (ed.), *Environmental Policies: An International Review*, London, Croom Helm, 1986, pp.45–8.

10 Such weariness is evident in C. Pye-Smith and C. Rose, *Crisis and Conservation*, Harmondsworth, Penguin, 1984.

11 J. Galtung *et al.*, 'Why the concern with ways of life?' in I. Miles and J. Irvine (eds), *The Poverty of Progress*, Oxford, Pergamon, 1983.

12 See the examples drawn from Scandinavian and Dutch experience in Miles and Irvine (eds), 1983, op. cit.

13 There is, thus, organisational and linguistic 'corruption' which are mutually, pathologically supportive and especially evident in the transnational institutions which both exploit and claim to control the use of natural resources.

14 H. Stretton, *Capitalism, Socialism and the Environment*, Cambridge, Cambridge University Press, 1976.

15 For an exceptionally clear account of this see M. Redclift, *Development and the Environmental Crisis: Red or Green Alternatives*, London, Methuen, 1984.

16 The early reports by Forester and by Meadows *et al.* (see chapter 6) depended upon the provision of reliable and expert data. It is true, however, that scientists and technologists who 'professionally' attack their employer industries are seen as deviant. See chapter 7 note 3.

17 The image of scientists does probably correspond to the universalism, disinterestedness, organised scepticism and disciplinary communism described by R.K. Merton, originally in 1942. See his *Social Theory and the Social Structure*, New York, Free Press, 1968, ch.XVIII. Much of the subsequent sociology of science has been an attempt to qualify this image.

18 On 'environmental impact assessment' see Holdgate, 1979, op. cit., pp.202–6; Redclift, 1984, op. cit., p.51; T. O'Riordan and R.D. Hey (eds), *Environmental Impact Assessment*, Farnborough, Saxon House, 1976.

19 W.A. Dando, *The Geography of Famine*, London, V.H. Winston/ Edward Arnold, 1980, p.XII.

20 This comment was made by P.K. Marstrand and H. Rush, 'Food and agriculture: when enough is not enough', in C. Freeman and M. Jahoda (eds), *World Futures: the Great Debate*, London, Martin Robertson, 1978. For a recent and relatively rare optimistic account see D.G. Johnson, 'World food and agriculture' in J.L. Simon and H. Kahn, (eds), *The Resourceful Earth: A Response to Global 2000*, Oxford, Blackwell, 1984. More generally see R. Bush, 'Unnatural disaster: the politics of famine', *Marxism Today*, vol.29, no.12, 1985, pp.8–11; *New Internationalist*, special issue, September 1985.

21 See P.N. Bradley, 'Food distribution and production', in R.J. Johnston and P.J. Taylor (eds), *A World in Crisis?*, Oxford, Blackwell, 1986.

22 FAO, *World Food Reports*, Rome, FAO, annually.

23 See Johnson, 1984, op. cit.

24 For instance S. George, *How the Other Half Dies*, Harmondsworth, Penguin, 1976; *Ill Fares the Land*, London, Writers and Readers, 1984; C. Robbins and J. Ansari, *The Profits of Doom*, London, War on Want, 1976; F.M. Lappe and J. Collins, *Food First*, London, Abacus, 1980.

25 For an acerbic view of the 'overpopulation myth' see George, 1976, op. cit., ch.2.

26 See R. Revelle, 'Resources available for agriculture', *Scientific American*, 1976, no.235, pp.164–78; Dando, 1980, op. cit., ch.6.

27 Marstrand and Rush, 1978, op. cit., pp.97–100.

28 Global 2000, *Report to the President of the US: Entering the 21st Century*, Oxford, Pergamon, 1980, summary volume, pp.94–120.

29 For general commentaries on the energy context see P. Odell, 'Draining the world of energy', in Johnston and Taylor (eds), 1986, op. cit.; J. Cheshire and K. Pavitt, 'Some energy futures', in Freeman and Jahoda (eds), 1978, op. cit. Opec raised the price of oil five-fold in 1973–4.

30 The obvious example is the current change of policy by the British Labour Party to a view favouring the phasing out of nuclear generation. For the instructive example of Sweden see M. Cross, 'Nuclear Sweden's final meltdown', *New Scientist*, vol. 110, no. 1509, 1986, pp.34–6.

31 See P. James, *The Future of Coal*, London, Macmillan, 1982; G. Foley, *The Energy Question*, Harmondsworth, Penguin, 1976.

32 Cheshire and Pavitt, 1978, op. cit., pp.119–20.

33 C. Sweet, *The Price of Nuclear Power*, London, Heinemann, 1983. The evidence given to the Sizewell inquiry is a rich source of data on the economic value of nuclear power. A useful digest of some of this information is provided, *inter alia*, in J. Valentine, *Atomic Crossroads*, London, Merlin Press, 1985 especially pp.49–65.

34 The official report on cancer 'clusters' around a particular power station did not have all the relevant data made available to it and this controversy continues. See the 'Black' Report, the Report of the Independent Advisory Group, *Investigation of the Possible Incidence of*

Cancer in West Cumbria, London, HMSO, 1984.
35 On low dose radiation effects see Valentine, 1985, op. cit., pp.158–72 for evidence to the Sizewell Inquiry, particularly that concerning Dr A. Stewart's study of childhood cancers, begun in the 1950s.
36 S. Kingman, 'A lot of fuss about a few millisieverts', *New Scientist*, vol.110, no.1108, 1986, p.26.
37 W.C. Patterson, *Nuclear Power*, Harmondsworth, Penguin, 1976, chs.6,7; Valentine, 1985, op. cit.; Z. Medvedev, 'Facts behind the Soviet nuclear disaster', *New Scientist*, vol.73, no.1058, pp.21–4, for an earlier Soviet accident in 1957–8.
38 There is not a great deal of readily available material on the Chernobyl incident. Following the reports in *New Scientist* from the first announcements of the disaster yields especially the following useful material; T. Wilkie and R. Milne, 'The world's worst nuclear accident', 1 May 1986; T. Wilkie, 'The unanswered questions of Chernobyl', 15 May, 1986; 'Chernobyl, the grim statistics of cancer', 14 August, 1986. Also see M. Hawkins *et al.*, *The Worst Accident in the World*, London, Pan, 1986. The journal *Nature*, especially during July and August 1986, provided a useful commentary and summary of official meetings and documents. The significant IAEA (International Atomic Energy Authority) Report on Chernobyl is summarised in *Nature*, 332, pp.672–3.
39 See D. Taylor, 'Chernobyl: the long-term consequences', *New Scientist*, vol.110, no.1508, 1986, p.24; W. Patterson, 'Why a kind of hush fell over the Chernobyl conference', *Guardian*, 4 October 1986.
40 A very clear account of these issues is given in Open University Course 201 – *Risk*, in Block 3 Unit 13 'Megarisks: Wagers on Doomsday', Milton Keynes, Open University Press, 1980. Also see J. Dowie and P. Lefrere (eds), *Risk and Chance*, Milton Keynes, Open University Press, 1980; K. Lindgren and S. Islam, 'How many reactor accidents will there be?', letter, *Nature*, 332, 1986, pp.691–2.
41 R. Jungk, *The Nuclear State*, London, Calder, 1979, ch.1.
42 H. Bacon and J. Valentine, *Power Corrupts*, London, Pluto Press, 1981.
43 See Sweet, 1983, op. cit., ch.2; Patterson, 1976, op. cit., ch.8.
44 What Sweet, ibid., ch.3, calls 'the institutional factor'.
45 Patterson, 1986, op. cit.
46 'Lifeboat ethics', popularised by G. Hardin, 'The Tragedy of the Commons', *Science*, vol.162, 1968, pp.1243–8; and *Ethics of a Lifeboat*, Washington, D.C., American Association for the Advancement of Science 1974, promotes the restriction of aid to the suffering on the grounds that the aid process itself reduces the security and stability of all. 'Triage' – a medical practice common in the World War I treatment of battle casualties – refers to the necessarily callous classification of the suffering into those who can and those who cannot be helped in the circumstances, and the abandonment of the latter to their fate.

CHAPTER 9 NEW MOVEMENTS?

1   See I. Miles and J. Irvine (eds), *The Poverty of Progress: Changing Ways of Life in Industrial Societies*, Oxford, Pergamon, 1983, p.9, note 1.

2   'Ah, but a man's reach should exceed his grasp/Or what's a Heaven for?', Robert Browning, 'Andrea del Sarto' from *Works of Robert Browning*, London, Smith and Elder, 1982.

3   A view clearly expressed in J. Keane, 'Surveillance State', *New Society*, 31 January, 1986, a review of A. Giddens, *The Nation State and Violence*, Cambridge, Polity Press, 1985. In the final chapters of this book Giddens gives an account of the significance of social movements as counter-influences to the increase in control and monitoring of the state. Keane locates hope significantly in these movements, much more so than Giddens.

4   This distinction is made by G. Day and D. Robbins, 'Activists for Peace: the social basis of a local peace movement', paper given to the British Sociological Association annual conference, University of Hull, 1984.

5   E. Laclau and C. Mouffe, *Hegemony and Socialist Strategy*, London, Verso, 1985, pp.159–70.

6   This begins with R. Michels' 'iron law of oligarchy' in *Political Parties*, Glencoe, Ill., Free Press, 1915.

7   For a useful bibliography of such movements across the world see M. Castells, *The City and the Grassroots*, London, Edward Arnold, 1983, pp.422–3, note 144.

8   See for instance B. Nedelmann, 'New political movements and changes in processes of intermediation', *Social Science Information*, vol.23. no.6, 1984, pp.1029–48.

9   See M. Olson, *The Logic of Collective Action*, Cambridge Mass., Harvard University Press, 1965 for public choice theory and J.D. McCarthy and M.N. Zald, 'Resource mobilization and social movements', *American Journal of Sociology*, vol.86, no.16. 1977, pp.761–4, for resource mobilisation theory.

10 A. Melucci, 'An end to social movements', *Social Science Information*, vol.23, no.4, 1984, pp.819–35.

11 P. Gundelach, 'Social transformation and new forms of voluntary associations', *Social Science Information*, vol.23, no.6, 1984, pp.1049–81. The notion of a 'new citizen' comes out clearly here.

12 A. Touraine *et al.*, *Anti-Nuclear Protest*, Cambridge, Cambridge University Press, 1983, p.179.

13 Castells, 1983, op. cit.; also see J.A. Hannigan, 'Alain Touraine Manuel Castells and social movement theory', *The Sociological Quarterly*, 1985, vol.26. no.4, pp.435–54.

14 S. Rowbotham *et al.*, *Beyond the Fragments*, London, Merlin, 1979.

15 Miles and Irvine (eds), 1983, op. cit.
16 The phantom of socio-biology lurks behind a great deal of social thought, and not just from the right. For an excellent general criticism of this meta-theory which should be long dead but won't lie down, see S.J. Gould, 'Cardboard Darwinism', *New York Review of Books*, vol.XXXIII, no.14, 1986, pp.47–54.
17 A. Maslow, *Motivation and Personality*, New York, Harper, 1954.
18 From many works see L. Kohlberg, 'Moral stages and moralization', in T. Lickona (ed.), *Moral Development and Behaviour*, New York, Holt, 1976.
19 R. Inglehart, *The Silent Revolution: Changing Values and Political Styles Among Western Publics*, Princeton J.J., Princeton University Press 1977.
20 H-U. Kohr and H-G. Rader (eds), *New Social Movements and the Perception of Military Threat in Western Democracies*, Munich, Sozialwissenschaftliches Institut der Bundeswehr, 1983; 'Generational learning, moral judgment and military threat', paper presented to the annual conference of the British Sociological Association, University of Hull, 1984.
21 See S. Cotgrove, *Catastrophe or Cornucopia*, Chichester, Wiley, 1982, chs.2,3, for this use of 'paradigm'.
22 See F. Parkin, *Middle Class Radicalism*, Manchester, Manchester University Press, 1968; R. Taylor and C. Pritchard, *The Protest Makers*, Oxford, Pergamon, 1980.
23 See N. Young, 'War resistance, state and society', in M. Shaw (ed.), *War, State and Society*, London, Macmillan, 1984 for this tradition.
24 Generally on the West German Greens see W. Hulsberg, 'Eco-Politics in West Germany', *New Left Review*, no.152, 1985, pp.5–29; F. Capra and C. Spretnak, *Green Politics*, London, Hutchinson, 1984; For some wider connections see *Journal of Peace Research*, special issue on peace movements, vol.23, no.2, 1986.
25 The West Germans have done considerable survey research on their youth, for instance the large study sponsored by Shell, 'Jugendwerk der Deutschen' *Lebensentwurfe, Alltagskulturen, Zukunftsbilder*, Opladen, Leske and Budrich, 1982.
26 P. Kelly, 'Strained Greens', interview, *Marxism Today*, vol.29, no.6, 1985, pp.15–19.
27 R. Bahro has sometimes been represented in Britain as *the* theoretician of the Greens. He represents only one faction, R. Bahro, *Socialism and Survival*, London, Heretic Press, 1982.
28 Parkin's view of CND was that it was a 'cause without an ideology', Parkin, 1968, op. cit., p.38.
29 See S. Elsworth, 'Staying clean in a dirty world', *Guardian*, 1 October 1986.
30 Castells, 1983, op. cit., ch.33 calls them 'reactive utopias'.

INDEX